Living On Purpose

Pat A. Paulson

Sharon C. Brown

Jo Ann Wolf

A Fireside Book
Published by Simon & Schuster Inc.
New York London Toronto Sydney Tokyo

Dedicated to Joe Durepos
who shares our vision

 Fireside
Simon & Schuster Building
Rockefeller Center
1230 Avenue of the Americas
New York, New York 10020

Copyright © 1988 by Phoenix Rising Press

First Fireside Edition, 1988

Published by arrangement with Phoenix Rising, Inc.

FIRESIDE and colophon are registered trademarks
of Simon & Schuster Inc.

Designed by Kathleen D. McCleave
Manufactured in the United States of America

1 3 5 7 9 10 8 6 4 2 Pbk.

Library of Congress Cataloging in Publication Data
Paulson, Pat A.
Living on purpose / Pat A. Paulson, Sharon C. Brown, Jo Ann Wolf.
—1st Fireside ed.
p.   cm.
A Fireside Book.
Reprint. Originally published: Glen Ellyn, IL : Phoenix Rising
Press, 1987.
ISBN 0-671-67223-1 Pbk.
1. Conduct of life.   2. Goal (Psychology)   3. New Age movement.
I. Brown, Sharon C.   II. Wolf, Jo Ann.   III. Title.
BJ1581.2.P37   1988
158′.1—dc19   88-11662
CIP

This book is not intended for use in psychotherapeutic
situations. All references to persons and places are fictitious
and any similarities to individuals living or dead are coincidental.

Contents

LIVING WITH PURPOSE

LIFE ENERGY

LIFE PURPOSE

LIFE WORK

The Beginning

We were friends with diversified back-grounds. We shared our joys, our troubles, and our thoughts. More than anything, we loved the way we could be together with new ideas. Whenever we met, we stayed up late, fascinated with each other's hopes and dreams. We all had similar but undefined goals. We wondered what we might do together in the world. We had moments when we would glimpse it, something we could do to make a difference. Evening after evening we spent together chasing ideas. It was invigorating. It was energizing. There was a notion hanging about, waiting for us to recognize it.

Our talks about life would lead us to a space. It was such a special space that we began to search for the big idea that created the space. Many evenings we got off on side trips, long ones, that led to dead ends. When we couldn't sustain energy on an idea, we knew to look elsewhere. We started hundreds of times in order to find what we did that created the space. We ate popcorn, burned hundreds of candles, and paced. What was this space?

Like other creators of ideas, we went through all kinds of motions to get this idea birthed. Sometimes we tried to force it. That didn't work. Sometimes we tried to ignore it. That didn't work. And then we got the idea that we were born for a Purpose. We recognized it, we felt its power and strength. We were filled. We knew that our Purpose lived in the space. Other great ideas began to take form that were unequivocal. We listened beyond our ears. Slowly, we got words to discuss these ideas with others. Did our ideas fit their lives? We talked about them constantly and the ideas evolved.

We glimpsed what we might do in the world together, and Phoenix Rising was born. The process lived. We picked and pulled every action and every behavior apart, scrutinizing our lives, and the lives of those we knew. We made the decision that we were going to share this material with others. We wondered what we were going to say. And through many years and many classes, we have decided that we do have something to share about the space. We are going to share a journey toward the space we call *Living On Purpose.*

Pat A. Paulson

Sharon C. Brown

Jo Ann Wolf

Introduction

Living On Purpose is about creating an experience in your life. It is an irreversible encounter with the person who lives inside, with your Purposed Self. It encourages you to claim *your* life, to live fully alive. It helps you remember what you may have forgotten, that you were born for something.

Living On Purpose is born of our intention to teach people to live their lives On Purpose. We wrote it to express our Life Purposes (Catalyst, Source, Teacher) and to teach you to find your own unique Life Purpose. This is a book to teach you what you already know. It will lighten, produce results, and give meaning to your life.

The material in this book will enable you to create for yourself the space of Purpose. It will teach you to know yourself and others without judgments. It will help you identify your Life Purpose and teach you what it means to live On Purpose. It will aid you in coming to choice about your Life Work. This material has been used by many people to facilitate their search for wholeness and purposefulness.

This book is about engaging with yourself. It asks you to be willing for a change, and it asks you to be intentional about your choices. You will want to turn your full attention to yourself and take your Purposed Self seriously. You will need to choose to take time for your own growth, making yourself the priority.

Living On Purpose can be read many ways. It can be read from beginning to end, from end to beginning, or from anywhere in between. Its content, and its order, will speak to different people differently. Use it in any order you want to. This is a book that can and will change your life if you read and work with it deliberately. You will find many ways to use this book. All ways are fine, and our experiences with people suggest that participating with the material as fully as possible increases its success.

Living On Purpose is designed to enhance and support the journey of your growth. It teaches you how to live On Purpose. Each chapter begins with an **Intention** that tells you what the chapter is meant to convey and where it will guide you. These Intentions are indexed at the back of the book for easy reference. The sections called **Talking About Life** present old ideas in new ways, enabling you to glean a different perspective about the content in your life. Most chapters have a **Story** to illustrate the information within the chapter. The **Comment** sections summarize what is in the text, while the **Big Idea**, a simple, easy to remember statement, helps underscore your awareness of the idea in each chapter. Questions or activities under **Your Life** will help you ponder the issues in your life that pertain to the material. Scattered throughout the book are single-page **Posters** that emphasize succinct ideas.

Living On Purpose is a guide that teaches you how to find yourself. Be generous with yourself as you read. Let this be your time. Set aside your concerns for awhile and participate with the material. This book was written to facilitate your search for Purpose so we invite you to keep reading and living, to love yourself and the process of your life, and to create your life anew by *Living On Purpose.*

Living With Purpose

Let It Light On You

Intention: To look at understanding

TALKING ABOUT LIFE

While you read this material, notice that your mind wants to understand it and has all kinds of reactions. You may think it easy or hard, new or old, boring or interesting, or a dozen other things. What you want to get is that the material presented here is about your living it, not understanding it. As you read and consider the material in this book, a greater *you* knows what you read. Get in touch with that knowing beyond understanding. Let it be. Let the words light on you. Just let this material get on you someplace for future reference as you live your life.

When you work in this material, do not think to the answers. You are waiting for answers from your Purposed Self. You want answers that startle you, ones that you feel at home with, ones that make you lighten up. Your mind may want to argue about the ideas you get, but you can let the answer be bigger than your mind. Your mind might tell you that *that* can't be the answer, because X, Y, and Z are so. Just tell your mind that you want to be with the ideas that come to you. You might want to try out a few ideas to see if they lighten you up. Your mind might also tell you that this doesn't make sense, and it doesn't want to read this anymore. So just keep reading anyway. The language of this book is designed to speak to you. Tell your mind you want to be with these words for awhile to see what lights on you.

STORY

Once a woman was having problems with her children. She had read somewhere that children often respond when you give them what they really want. Somewhere inside that information startled her. Her mind instantly jumped in with, "You can't do that! Think of the burden that will impose upon you. Your children will run your life with their demands. You will never have a moment and besides, you don't even agree with them. You know they are making a huge mistake, and they will want you to bail them out again."

The woman felt awful as she watched her relationships with her children deteriorate. She felt anxious and miserable not knowing what to do.

Suddenly, she got an idea. She began wondering what in the world her children really wanted from her. When she thought about it, she realized more than anything else they wanted her approval about the ways they were choosing to live their lives. She wondered what she would have to give up in order to approve of her children's lives. Immediately she realized it would take almost no effort on her part and consequently she felt lighter. Then she remembered about something she had read that she hadn't understood at the time, yet someplace inside she "knew" it. The information lit on her.

COMMENT

When you struggle to understand something, it diminishes the usefulness of the information. Much understanding occurs in the process of living life. When it's applicable, it's applicable. When it's not, it's not. That's all.

THE BIG IDEA
You will gather much more information when you don't reject it with your mind and you just let it light on you.

Have you ever had the experience of an idea lighting on you?

What outrageous idea did you previously hear about that you are now living?

How could you benefit if you let information light on you?

Do you have a habit of needing to understand everything?

To Live Deliberately

Intention: To focus on the moments

TALKING ABOUT LIFE

The richness of life unfolds as you realize that a full life is made up of living every moment. When you give yourself permission to get into the moments of your life, you begin to know the meaning of deliberation. You understand that there are few accidents in your life. You experience a momentum that is wanting to guide you somewhere. It's not unlike a subtle force aligning you with the life that you were born to live. You become aware that there is a definite path to follow toward a definite goal. The path seems unfamiliar to you but challenges you with signs of great lightness about your life. You never lose sight of the goal as the path disappears behind you and the only way to proceed is forward toward the unknown goal. The moment of life becomes your focus even though the purpose may not be understood.

Throughout your development you have been told to live a "good" life. You have come to understand that goodness is born of compassion and charity toward yourself and others. Your life has meaning, and all of your encounters, whether they are with your inner self or with others, make a difference. The wonder of living

If you want to trade your life,

you must trade

the whole thing.

a good life is that it challenges you to live deliberately with the focus of attention on your greater purpose. The most deliberate you can ever live is to let your unique purpose be your guide.

Your purpose guides you toward a rich life that, once expressed, often creates an irreversible encounter with yourself and others. Once you accept the challenge of living On Purpose, you must accept the responsibility that your purpose *does* make a difference. This acceptance brings you to the choice of living a good deliberate life or living randomly, but you may never again pretend that you have no choice.

Therefore you stretch yourself to honor the purpose of your life, giving yourself over to each new concept that presents itself. Living deliberately is not living without inconvenience. However, you learn that the inconvenience you experience is itself a teacher. Once you accept the inconvenience, you have made the choice to live so much more of your life. Your view of your life and how you can live it expands and you find yourself once again further along the path toward the unknown goal with more passion to live each moment.

Living deliberately requires the knowledge that you have a purpose. It demands that you examine the content of your life and glean the message it holds for you.

STORY

Shortly before his death, a Lama confided to a nun that he planned to reincarnate as the child of a woman he knew. A year later, this woman did have a son. She hadn't known of the Lama's intent, but all signs pointed to the fact that her son was the Lama reincarnated.

People gathered and a religious ceremony was performed and solemn offerings were bestowed upon him. The mother is deliberate about raising this son, until he leaves, at eight years of age, to live in a monastery. She will raise him in a peaceful place of pure energy in order to develop his mind quickly.

COMMENT

When you realize that you are on the path of your life's journey, it is too late to retrace your steps. You may choose to stay stuck and not grow, but even that becomes so uncomfortable that you are compelled to move.

THE BIG IDEA

You get the most you can get from life when you are deliberate about your choices for living. You need to notice the moment to make this possible.

In what content area are you now living deliberately, noticing the moments that help guide you?

Describe some of the choices you made in the past and how they got you further along your path.

How can you remember to be deliberate in choice making?

Notice the moment.
Stay in the Present.

How have you stretched yourself to live deliberately?

What have you learned about the moments of
your life?

*Becoming aware of each
moment makes it Full*

Do the moments of living count for you?   In
what way?

When was a time you got off the path toward
your goal?

Life Is Your Process

Intention: To love what happens

TALKING ABOUT LIFE

Does it ever happen that you dislike your life so much that you want a completely different life? Whose life would you want to live? Whose life would be better for you? Your life is actually the perfect one for you.

When you look back on your life you can begin to see that life is a process. The process is a journey through content that has inspired you to grow and mature. The process has been an opportunity for you to learn and stretch yourself physically, emotionally, and mentally. You are in the process of your own personal evolution.

Your relationships are in process. Your job is in process. Your education is in process. To be in process means that you are living. You notice that your life looks different than it did five years ago. You feel differently about the things in your life. You know more, and you experience it differently. You are moving and living in your process.

Those times that you hate your process, or you want to skip a particular part, or you are afraid of the content are the times you are denying the natural process of your life. If the content was not there for you to look at and experience, why would it have arrived in your life?

It arrived in your life because your process yesterday determines your process today. What you refused to live has not gone away, it has only taken a different form. The content of your life is only finished when it is no longer applicable to your process. When there is content you refuse to live, you are trying to skip over an important opportunity for growth, knowledge, and personal evolution. The lie is that you can skip some piece of content that has arrived in your life. Skipping over content only brings different content with exactly the same kind of worry, concern, and consideration.

The ideal way to live is to love and trust your process. If you decide to like where it takes you, it never really takes you any place you don't want to go. The love and trust you bring to your process is the same love and trust you bring to yourself, your life. You don't really make mistakes in your process. You can judge it all you want. You can make your process wrong, you can try to control it, and most of all you can try to change it mid-experience, but the truth is that you are in this life to live it fully. There is a whisper inside of you that calls you to love your life. It calls you to respect your process because you are the one with the inner wisdom that has asked for growth and evolution.

You don't want your life to stop living itself. Your process is totally about you. It is about you wanting to be all you can be in your life. What else is there to do? Halting your process or refusing to live it has not gained you happiness ever after. The instant you embrace your process you are making the statement that you are willing and ready to live. You are saying that you love your life and that you will continue to live it even if you aren't sure how.

When you trust your process, it seems as if a

power and wisdom larger than yourself begins to guide and help you. You become a receiver for your process to lead you to your mission. Your process is yours and yours alone. No one else can experience the significance of it or interpret it for you. It is your life made up of content that is your process. You must decide. You must live it.

STORY

A woman was enjoying a quiet suburban life. The home she created for herself was comfortable and it expressed her charm. She was successful and experienced great pleasure from her career. People loved her company and she had a satisfying social life. Occasionally she traveled, enjoying the discovery of new places. Not many problems found her because she guarded her content meticulously.

She studied esoteric wisdom, assimilating select knowledge that enhanced her life. One interest that fascinated her was people and how they live their lives. She became an expert at teaching others what they needed to learn. An observer could only conclude that she was living the perfect life.

However, a subtle discontent began churning. Not exactly knowing why, she travelled on a yearlong trip. She didn't return the same, but she was unaware of the irreversible changes taking place within her. She had expected to return to her familiar, prosaic life, but her carefully guarded content was no longer satisfying. Something inside was calling and she didn't understand what it might be. It seemed strange to her that she couldn't settle down into the comfort of her life. She began to wonder about what experiences she was missing. Month after month found her searching for answers to undefinable questions.

Her search took her places she never expected to be. Slowly, the light began to dawn. She believed she had a Purpose that wasn't being fulfilled. Effort and struggle dogged her when she rejected change. Some of the content that arrived for her to do went against her logical judgment. Often she wasn't interested in going the same direction her life was headed.

It happened that she was finding herself out on a limb. Her friends and other influential people sometimes questioned her good judgment. However, each time she took a new step that honored her process, she experienced greater satisfaction.

Today she is highly respected and her knowledge is in great demand. Her courage to take the risks her life process demands has led her on a journey of personal growth and major contribution.

COMMENT

When you realize that your life is your process, you can honor this process above all. You know that you have a whole life to consider when making decisions. You want to nourish and respect your whole life while doing whatever shows up in your life to do. When you love your process, you give yourself permission to look at your life and your needs as a whole.

THE BIG IDEA

Your life is your process, and when you love it you love yourself. You have a much larger vision of yourself and what is important in your growth.

What parts of your process do you love the most?

What parts of your process do you dislike the most?

What parts of your process would you like to skip?

What parts of your process have you denied?

What parts of your process are you creating now?

All The World's Your Stage

Intention: To see the acts of your life

TALKING ABOUT LIFE

In the course of your life, you do many things and play many roles. You know that over the course of time all of the content of your life changes. What you were interested in years ago no longer claims your attention. For a moment, rerun your life like a movie. Rewind the film to various scenes. Run it in regular motion. Run it in fast motion. Run it in slow motion.

There are scenes where you are the star, the leading performer—the heroine, the hero, the vamp, the villian, the boss, the parent, whomever. You are the strong one, saving the day for family and friends. You are the troublemaker, around whom all the action swirls. You have played almost all of the leading roles in different movies of your life. There are some scenes where you have walk-on parts or parts with few lines. You will notice that in your life you have played many parts, in many scenes, in many different plays.

And, you will also notice that at times you played your part with passion, with earnestness, no matter what the lines. You were involved. You were alive, whether with joy or sadness. You played it as if it were your only perfor-

All the world's your stage.

You have the leading role.

mance, which, in fact, you will now notice that it was.

And you will also notice that there were many times that your performance was that of an amateur, awkward and reluctant, forced into the play because another player was needed, wanting to hide behind the curtains, wanting to say that this play was not yours. Uttering your lines without meaning, without feeling, without involvement. Without heart.

Realizing that you are not the drama you are in at the moment, that you are larger than any particular piece of content, is a necessary step in coming to know who you really are. The dramas of our lives can sometimes be so intense that they convince us that we *are* them. But, looking back, even the worst of the dramas is upstaged by the next production.

STORY

A woman with little job preparation was caught in a difficult scenario of being financially responsible for herself and her two children. She was overwhelmed by her lack of prospects. However, when she looked back at her life, she realized that there had been other tough scenes that she had lived through, which she had come to value as a part of her whole process. She decided that to view her current situation as the whole of her life brought her to self-doubts and despair. However, when she saw her current life situation as only one scene of her life, she was able to go through the details without despair. Although the facts of her life did not immediately change, her ability to view the situation as only one piece of the whole changed her experience.

COMMENT

Sometimes the content of the life you are living is so compelling and demanding that you lose sight of the idea that this is but one scene of the whole play called "Your Life." In the course of your life, you will be in many dramas, playing many parts. Remembering this will lighten your experience of the scenes of your life.

THE BIG IDEA

All the world's your stage.
You have the leading role.

Consider your life as a drama, identifying the scenes and the roles you played in them. Use a star rating, with **** being excellent and * being boring.

One of the scenes of the *first significant act* of my life was:

I held the following positions (check them):

    __Lead Performer
    __Supporting Performer
    __Director
    __Editor
    __Producer
    __Set Designer
    __Not Sure
    __Other

I rate the act ___. I rate my performance___.

One of my *greatest roles* was in a play called:

Where I played the part of:

Briefly tell what the part included, why you liked it or why you didn't like it. What was the most memorable scene and line?

I held the following positions:

__Lead Performer
__Supporting Performer
__Director
__Editor
__Producer
__Set Designer
__Not Sure
__Other

I rate the act ___. I rate my performance___.

One time I was *drafted* into a play called:

Where I played the part of:

Briefly tell what the part included, why you liked it or why you didn't like it.

I held the following positions:

__Lead Performer
__Supporting Performer
__Director
__Editor
__Producer
__Set Designer
__Not Sure
__Other

I rate the act ___. I rate my performance___.

I am currently playing in:

Where I play the part of:

Briefly tell what the major issues are in the current play.

I hold the following positions:

__Lead Performer
__Supporting Performer
__Director
__Editor
__Producer
__Set Designer
__Not Sure
__Other

I rate the act ___. I rate my performance___.

Briefly tell whether you've been in this play before, whether you're playing full-out, whether you love being in this play.

I will be nominated for awards in the following categories:

I will win awards in the following categories:

Who Are The Thurmans?

Intention: *To lighten up*

TALKING ABOUT LIFE

Grenelda and Herman Thurman are the roy-
alty of randomnicity. She will do anything, any-
time. He says yes without thinking. She is the
one running your life when you are not paying
attention. He jumps in and does any-old-thing.
Life seems out of control, and she is buffeted by
whatever and whomever's content shows up.
Mediocre turns bad and bad turns worse.

You really were not in your right mind when
trouble arrived. Grenelda or Herman was running the show. So there you are, trouble all
around. What happens? You get down on yourself for not running your life. The overall feeling
is heavy, and from this place it is hard to get a
shift out of the downward spiral. All the heaviness just adds to the downward movement.
Where is the deliberateness of your choices about
living?

Grenelda Thurman volunteered another
time for another project that you have come to
hate. Herman Thurman got in the car behind
the steering wheel and drove off in the wrong
direction. Grenelda put down your keys when
you came home so that now you can't find them
anywhere. Herman does not have your best in-

terest at heart. He is not malicious, just without Purpose.

Actually, they are a little humorous and when you can step back and say, "Oh, it was the Thurmans who stepped in and made all this mess," you can lighten up about yourself. It is this lightening up that creates the possibility of your shifting. Sometimes thinking about the Thurmans can create laughter, whereas without them you would be making great negative judgments about yourself. It is easy to see that the possibility for improving the situation is more likely to live in laughter than judgment.

STORY

Herman Thurman says yes to two conflicting events on the same day.

Grenelda Thurman opens her mouth and speaks randomly.

Herman Thurman volunteers your time when you have none.

Grenelda Thurman speaks to people and never hears what they are saying.

Herman Thurman flies into rages and slips into depressions.

COMMENT

When you notice that your life has fallen into disarray, instead of getting angry at yourself and making yourself wrong, remember the Thurmans. They are a lighthearted way of getting some lightness in your life.

> ### THE BIG IDEA
>
> Lightening up creates possibility, while heaviness, guilt, and depression foster immobility.

What has Herman Thurman said yes to that you didn't want to do?

What did Grenelda Thurman forget to do that you wanted to do?

What mood did Herman Thurman fall into that you didn't want to be in?

What times does Grenelda show up most?

Living On Purpose

TALKING ABOUT LIFE

One interesting phenomenon in life is the experience of reality. Reality is associated with interpreting experiences that create belief systems. And these experiences vary dramatically. One person's experience is often the opposite of another's, and there are innumerable judgments about the same issues. Just consider governments and religion. One group believes in totalitarianism and another in democracy; one in religion, and others in atheism.

Other issues also have discrepancies in reality. Think of couples facing the decisions of career versus family, natural foods versus convenience foods, more education versus less education, or medicine versus natural healing, for example.

Ask yourself what judgments you have and what realities you oppose. The input you receive daily challenges your reality. You can believe an experience, such as losing your job, was the worst thing that ever happened to you, only to discover it was the best thing that ever happened. Your biggest challenge here is to be aware of yourself, and to choose as your reality those positions that will enhance your personal evolution.

You decide.

Personality

or

On Purpose?

The clarity with which you interpret your experience will be your greatest tool for choosing your reality. If you interpret an experience from your emotions, or define it from your mind, you will have fewer options about your life. A good example of this is choosing never to trust someone again because they once betrayed you. Maybe this experience was ten years ago and now there is evidence of their total trustworthiness, but your experience was so devastating you won't believe in them. The experience of a strong emotion has decided your reality. A different example is reading about nutrition in an offbeat magazine that appeals to your logic. Perhaps you were persuaded that all you ever need to eat is sunflower seeds. Maybe one sentence captured your mind, so you've just spent the last three weeks eating seeds and feeling awful. But your mind is made up, and you believe that good health is just around the corner.

These are examples of choosing reality from experiences that are controlled by emotions and mind; most of your reality is determined just this way. This is allowing your personality to determine your reality. You have come to believe that you *are* your body, your emotions, and your mind. Does it really matter that you are too short? Are you less of a human being because of your physical stature, or can you imagine that your body is not you, it is just your vehicle? If your arm is amputated, are *you* diminished?

Or maybe you believe that you are your emotions? Have you decided that you will never use your natural ability to comfort because you are too shy and nervous around people? Do you believe your mind is too sophisticated to waste on teaching people to grow corn in underdeveloped countries, even though it is your secret desire to do so?

Letting your personality determine your reality will always diminish your experience of yourself. Your personality was developed by input it received long before you recognized choice; it has judgments concerning most of your experiences. Some things it believes are good, others bad; some right, some wrong; some best, some worst; and, of course, it believes you should or you shouldn't. These dualities limit you. Maybe your mind believes you shouldn't do the very thing that would bring you great satisfaction. Or you guard yourself, limiting your experience so you will only have good emotions. Your personality has major judgments that overtly and subtlely control you.

Who is in charge of your life and who is determining your reality? You may believe you are, but if your personality, with all of its judgments, is in charge, you can't know who is running your life. For instance, you might make a decision because your family has always done it that way, not because it fits for you. Who decided their way is the best way? Who is in charge? The only way for *you* to get in charge of your life is to notice your judgments. As you notice your judgments, you will see that they moderate who you want to be. Contrary to what you may have been thinking, your judgments *are* your limitations. When you allow your judgments to determine your reality, you are living within the boundaries they create. Sadly, your judgments may not even be yours. The world is saturated with judgments, and you have probably adopted some that caught your mind.

The only way to experience a new reality is to give up your judgments. You will know instantly when you have, because your experience will be clear and your reality will be freeing. You will have transformed your reality to living On Purpose. You will have no trouble recognizing it. First, you will realize that you do not have an opinion about the issue that you once had strong judgments about. You will feel lighter, as if some burden has been lifted. Or, you may finally experience a peace that you have been seeking. It could be an overwhelming sense of fulfillment, but whatever it is you will know that a shift has occurred in what you believe. You will realize that you are not experiencing the same way: you are in a different space.

When living On Purpose is your *focus*, you experience each event as an original happening. You know what is about the moment. Your mind is not rushing to compare experiences so you can make up some judgment about them. Your emotions are quiet; therefore you are not alarmed. You have no one to blame because you are not a victim.

It may feel risky to you to give up a judgment that has been part of your identity. Your major concerns, such as governments, religion, and health become your responsibility, and you decide the extent of your involvement. Other concerns become your responsibility also, as you decide your needs and how to fulfill them.

Living On Purpose is a *choice* about choosing your reality. When you set aside your judgments you will see what is. No one is doing anything to you. That is what is. They are simply doing what they are doing. As long as you judge them as doing something right or wrong, you are trapped as a victim. You are a victim of their wrong doing, or you are a victim of their righteousness.

Living On Purpose has two requirements: giving up your judgments and getting what is. A different reality is born when you create these conditions. To test it, all you need to do is give up one judgment and notice what happens. You will be at choice; now you can choose what makes you feel lighter, empowered, at peace, or whatever you want. But it will be what *you* want, not what is best, or right, or should be, or any other way your mind and emotions have previously controlled you. It is an exciting reality, one that gives you yourself. One where you will find joy to be alive.

Living On Purpose is a *process*. You have so many judgments, you can't instantly identify them all. However, each time you give one up, you have changed your reality from living in your personality to living On Purpose. You have a greater experience of yourself. It is a process of living each day to see yourself and the judgments you have. Where do you feel limited? Where do you want more space to live? What judgments can you let go of, and what choices will you make when you see what is?

More than any other thing, you want to live *your* life, the one that means something to you. You know inside what makes you feel great. Make those choices, no matter what your previous judgments have been. Look forward to discovering your judgments and the challenge of giving them up. You will be creating a new reality for yourself. It is described as Living On Purpose.

STORY

A young girl was a victim of incest. The ramifications pervaded her entire life. She was incorrigible, even suicidal at times. Her education suffered because she was unable to concentrate and she defied authority. Her behavior was so belligerent at home that everyone fought with her.

She was young, with long golden hair and soft blue eyes, but she hated the way she looked and she believed she was ugly. Inside, she had a gentle nature about her, and the times she could relax she showed a remarkable interest in caring for people. Most times, however, she despised being asked to help and openly refused to do so. Actually, she hated to see anyone suffer, yet she would find herself physically battling with her siblings and friends.

Education was another contradiction. She was intelligent and curious, yet failure plagued her. Secretly she loved school and learning, but her inability to concentrate was her great nemesis. She was, in fact, living a life of victimhood.

Her mother had been informed by professionals that victims of incest were hopeless. The psychological damage is so great they can never overcome it. This girl's mother searched constantly for help for her daughter. She never stopped believing that some day her daughter would experience emotional healing. Her mother understood that the girl's interpretation of her experience was creating her reality. She was determined to help her daughter shift her reality.

They were hardly able to endure the emotional pain. The mother struggled with every position, trying to communicate with the young girl. The girl had lived so much life in her few short years, it seemed she would always live with extreme hardship. She moved from one relationship to another, all of them supporting her low opinion of herself.

One day a miracle happened. The first news of the intervention didn't seem like a miracle at all. The girl was pregnant and planning to keep her baby. Knowing her emotional instability caused everyone to be gravely concerned. However, something was happening inside the girl. She was examining her life and her behavior, because she wanted this baby more than she had ever wanted anything. She made major changes, ones that didn't defeat her. Her first concern, in the creation of a new reality, was what she wanted for herself and her baby. Many times she didn't know how it was going to work, but she believed she would make it work.

She began by giving up her severe judgments of herself, and she no longer invited other's negative judgments. Her successes were adding up. During a long conversation, the girl looked her mother straight in the eyes and said, "Never again refer to me as a victim. I am going to look forward to my life. No matter what anyone says, I believe I can make it."

COMMENT

Choosing a reality is claiming your experience as what is. No one else lives your life. Don't let them interpret your experience. Anything less than that leaves you living a reality that may have nothing to do with who you are. You decide what it means for you to live On Purpose.

THE BIG IDEA

The way to Live On Purpose is to give up your judgments and get what is. Give them up one at a time and each time you will be at choice to react from your personality or On Purpose.

What judgments do you have that are creating a reality that you don't want?

What emotions are controlling your reality?

What logic is controlling your reality?

What time did you know you were at choice about your experience?

What reality did you choose then—personality or On Purpose?

How was it different than other choices you have made?

What reality do you presently have that you would like to change?

What judgments do you need to give up?

What judgments are you going to give up?

Judgments Galore

Intention: To identify your judgments

TALKING ABOUT LIFE

Judgments are as much a part of you as breathing. You have judgments about everything. You believe your judgments matter. Your judgments are about yourself, your content, others and their content, and the world at large. You have blatant judgments and obscure judgments. You have small and petty judgments and large and paralyzing judgments. It's almost as if your mind waits for you to think any thing just so it can judge it.

Judgments are different than making decisions. In the larger scope of life you will notice that you make many decisions. You may even be afraid to make decisions. The fear about decisions comes from your judgments. You have predetermined whether your decisions are the right or wrong ones. You may look at your past history and judge that you never make good decisions or that things don't turn out when you make decisions. The decisions are not the problem; your judgments about them are what cause the anxiety.

It is very difficult to live life and not have judgments. It will not work to tell yourself, "I will never judge anything again." Just notice what your judgment is when you are stuck or

*The fewer
your
judgments,
the larger
your life.*

Living On Purpose

feeling bad and then see if you can let it go. Do it in the moment of your experience, and you will have accomplished much. The more you are On Purpose, the more you can let your content be what it is. Notice yourself and what you have judgments about first. Notice how you won't do X or associate with Z because you have a strong judgment. You probably are not aware of the immediate or long range effects of these judgments, but that does not alter the fact that they do affect you. The more judgments you keep, the more constricted is the space in which you live.

Giving up your judgments may feel like you are giving up your identity. In a way you are. You are making a statement that says, "I want to live larger than my judgments. I want to live greater than my present personality." Some judgments are not even your own. They have been imposed upon you as something that is correct to believe, think, or feel. To truly expand your life, you must come from a premise different than your present way of judging things.

You must let go and let your Purposed Self guide you. It is risky and often there is no road map and no evidence. But you will move along toward the life that you know you are meant to live.

STORY

A middle-aged man had very definite opinions about life. He strongly believed that once he married it would be forever. He accumulated all the things that he believed would insure a wonderful life. He had a good job, a wonderful home, and two children that he was proud of. His wife was a sweet person who almost never disagreed with him.

A flaw in his life was a job requirement that he occasionally travel. One time his assignment took him to a distant city for several weeks. Night after night he had dinner alone at the same restaurant and it was beginning to bother him.

One evening he invited a woman colleague to have dinner with him. He just didn't want to be alone again. He was surprised to discover how much he enjoyed her company. So he invited her again and then again.

When the travel assignment was over, he returned home but he could not forget the woman. He made arrangements to see her again. They had fallen in love. He hoped to keep it a secret but the situation accelerated. They decided they wanted to spend their lives together. Despite his judgments about marriage being forever, he got a divorce.

Now he is unhappy. He still has a judgment that when you marry it is forever. Even though he is married to his new love, he can't get his former life off his mind.

COMMENT

When you appreciate what is, you are preparing yourself for the miracles that are just around the corner. When you judge what is, you are blind to the joys of the moment.

THE BIG IDEA

The fewer your judgments, the larger your life.

What judgments are you presently holding that contract the space you want to live in?

What small shift can you make about these judgments?

Get a shift in one judgment and write about your experience. How did it feel inside?

What has manifested in your life since giving up this judgment?

In the future, what are the clues that can help you notice a disabling judgment?

What judgments do others have about you?

What judgments do you need?

What is your list of small and petty judgments?

The Difference

TALKING ABOUT LIFE

When you think about your life, you will notice that you have judgments, you have opinions, and you make decisions. You will want to become aware of how you think about yourself and others. And you will need to differentiate between thinking that liberates you and thinking that limits you.

Examination of your judgments will show you that there is a basic problem—you can be convinced that you are your judgments. Judgments are *firm positions* you insist upon whether or not they continue to be relative to the issue you are judging. For example, you believe that you can never have the job of your dreams because you don't have the credentials. Then someone informs you that they just accepted your dream job, and they have no experience or credentials.

Maybe you have made the judgment that intelligent people have an education. You don't have that education; therefore you believe you are not intelligent. Or it could be a small and petty judgment, such as short people cause trouble. What if you have missed out on the perfect relationship because you avoid short people?

Decisions are just decisions.

Period.

Opinions, on the other hand, are different from judgments. Your opinions are your *preferences*. Definitely you have opinions about the content in your life. You may have an opinion that your children need to go to college. You prefer that they have an education. However you don't stop loving them and you don't judge them as unsuccessful if they don't. Or maybe you have an opinion that it is better to live in a warm climate. You prefer long hot days. But you don't divorce your lifelong partner when they are transferred to Alaska. And maybe you have opinions about certain addictions. Are you going to avoid or stop caring about your best friend if they start smoking again?

The question may be whether you need judgments to make responsible decisions about your life. What if you decide to move across the country and it doesn't work out? Do you continue to struggle trying to make it work or do you make another decision to move back? If you make a judgment that it was irresponsible to move, you will damage your self-esteem. However, if you have an opinion that it isn't working out, you can easily decide what you prefer.

Decisions are just decisions, period. When you base your decisions on judgments, they will be self-defeating. When you base your decisions on your opinions, you can change them to fit your preferences.

You will want to stay aware about your opinions. If you are gathering evidence so you can keep your opinions, they will not be preferences much longer. They are quickly becoming judgments that will limit you.

When you want to live On Purpose you will differentiate between judgments, opinions, and decisions. Your opinions will give you the space to be flexible and make many decisions. You can decide one way and then the opposite way. You are simply following your preferences. You will enjoy the responsibility of your choices because they are based upon your opinions.

If you have an opinion that your children should go to college, you will not consider it a great sacrifice to keep driving your old car or to forego your vacations to save money for this expense. You accept your responsibility because you have this preference. Depending on the decisions you and your children make, you may change your preference.

Your judgments always limit you because you must live within the fixed boundaries of them. When you judge that something is wrong, you force yourself to avoid content that would challenge your judgment. When you know the difference, you may want to consider what judgments you have that could become opinions.

STORY

A young woman was interested in meeting someone with whom she could develop a serious relationship. She had fixed judgments about how this person should be. She wanted someone who was a nonsmoker, vegetarian, and intellectual. This someone had to love classical music and long bike rides on the weekends. Also, this someone had to be at least six feet tall because she was five feet ten inches tall herself.

She had dates with different people but there was always some thing that disappointed her. Then her friend introduced her to someone she was attracted to. They dated; their relationship became serious. She believed she had found the perfect person because he fit her judgments of the perfect person. Everything was fine. Then one day, he gave up his vegetarian interests.

Some of the judgments you have are opinions that you became married to. A judgment gives you one position about the issue. You are not free to make other decisions. An opinion is a preference that you keep deciding about.

THE BIG IDEA

The difference is between liberation and limitation. If your judgments can become opinions you will be set free.

What opinions do you have about your relationships?

What judgments do you have about your relationships?

What opinions do you have about yourself?

What judgments do you have about yourself?

What decisions have you made based on your opinions?

What decisions have you made based on your judgments?

Why You Want To
Live On Purpose

Intention: To choose to live On Purpose

TALKING ABOUT LIFE

Living On Purpose is a choice. It is a way of living in which you are at choice about each moment of each day. Every situation presents you with a new opportunity to decide how you will be about it. You can choose from many different positions how you will act or react to any content that is present in your life. No one else can ever decide for you how you will be. No one can get inside you and advise or demand that you should be one way or the other. It is always your choice.

You have made many choices about living, and you have made those choices for many reasons. Sometimes you chose to live On Purpose because there was no other way to choose. Sometimes you thought you were not at choice. Maybe an emotion captured you and you found yourself at the effect of that emotion for a long period of time. Maybe your mind led you into believing that if you lived a certain way you would be happy. You struggled to live the way your mind insisted, yet you didn't find happiness. Maybe all you ever wanted to do was just get by, have a quiet life in the suburbs without too much trouble, and somehow trouble persisted in

Be generous

to yourself.

Live

On Purpose.

finding you. Maybe you chose to get all you could from life and now you have it, and still you find you are missing something.

All of these examples are choices about how you want to live and experience life. Choosing to live On Purpose is a statement about your life. You are stating that deliberate living is going on. It is a choice that declares that you are intent about your life. Living On Purpose positions you to live and express yourself in a way that aligns you with the idea that you were born for something. You are not living a life that has no purpose, nothing to contribute.

Living On Purpose simply means becoming aware enough of living so that you are at choice about your experience and what you want to do. You notice your content and your experience of your content, and you get yourself to choice about it. You may choose to experience it emotionally but at least you have chosen. You may think about content in a particular way, but you have chosen to think about it that way. You can decide to think and experience in a way that lightens the situation for you. You will not be controlled by some mysterious feeling or thought pattern that you no longer remember, because you know what is and you are at choice.

Living On Purpose will ask you to think in new ways about yourself. You will come to love how you are and how you do. You will live your life knowing what you are doing. You will find inner peace and fulfillment. You will also contribute to your relationships and the world at large because it makes a difference when you respond with the intention to make it count. You will feel good about yourself and others because you are not thinking or expecting them to behave in any particular way.

You will want to live On Purpose as an expression of your greatest self. And you will want to live On Purpose because there just isn't any other real way to live. Everything, everywhere is calling you to choose a way to live that makes you feel light. The opportunities are endless because you keep creating new opportunities that challenge you to live On Purpose or not.

STORY

When people lose someone they love there is a natural grieving process. Emotions can be devastating and sometimes people think they cannot live with this loss.

It may seem as if life isn't fair, or the pain is too great to continue, or that there is nothing else to live for. Minds and emotions have all kinds of responses to get you to a position that alleviates the pain. These responses rarely encourage you to take giant steps toward a life beyond the pain of loss. But there comes a time when you must find a new way to have loss in your life and still continue living.

This is the time to come to choice about your life and how you want to live. You must take the first step of deciding that your life is worth the experience of living. Then there will be another step and another and you keep living all the steps. There will come a moment when you realize your life is expanding and you are living with loss and pain and you are still living. Finally the moment will come and you will realize that you are really living magnificently, deliberately, and at choice.

You want to live On Purpose because it is about your life.

You want to live On Purpose because you get more out of your life.

You want to live On Purpose because it lightens you.

You want to live On Purpose because you have inner peace.

You want to live On Purpose because you contribute when you do.

You want to live On Purpose because ultimately there is nothing else to do.

THE BIG IDEA

You have the choice to live moment to moment On Purpose.

Practice developing your awareness of how you live by taking a moment to breathe before you automatically respond.

What have you noticed about this?

List some of the benefits you might receive by choosing to live On Purpose.

List some of the times you handled yourself in a way that was uniquely you, when all you had to go on was a choice about how you were going to be.

List new ways of looking at old content that would lighten it for you.

Who Gets Up In The Morning?

Intention: To get up on your side

TALKING ABOUT LIFE

When does your day start? Are you the one who wakes up eager for another day and anxious to begin it? Or are you the one whose day doesn't start until after the first coffee break? Or perhaps you don't start your day until after lunch.

The important thing about starting your day is to get to choice about how you are going to use it. That is what the start is about; it is about getting into your own life, the life you want to live. You want to get into your life as soon as you can. You want to choose as quickly as you can to live the moments you are living.

Notice how you get out of bed. Take a few moments for yourself and notice how you are feeling about your life. Notice what you are thinking about your life. If you don't like where you are, can you find a way to shift it, so your experience of living the day will be more to your liking? Be generous to yourself for a few moments when you first get up.

The trouble with not noticing and not getting into your life as soon as you can is that, if you haven't paid attention and you wander into the kitchen and someone says "Good morning," you are likely to inflict your mood on them. You know that how you are affects other people, so you want it to be a good mood. You know the truth of the expression, "You got up on the wrong side of the bed." It's because you forgot to notice who gets out of bed. Your day starts when you get up. Get up on the side you want, into the life you want.

The reason you want your day to start when you awake is because it contributes to the quality of your life. You are in your life for more of the moments of your life. You can't assume that you will get up on the side you want. You can't assume that you will get up in your life. Get up deliberately.

STORY

One day while on vacation a woman woke up and immediately argued with her children about the events of the day. She was surprised, because she had previously intended that the most important thing about the vacation was having a wonderful time with her children. She had decided not to fight the daily battles about vegetables and bedtime. She intended to create a wonderful vacation. She had told the children that this was a special time in their lives, and up to that point the vacation had been wonderful. Just the evening before, they had planned the events of the next day.

When morning came and they all got up, however, she forgot that her intention about the vacation was to have a wonderful time. She forgot the conversation of last night and she entered a tug of wills with her children, arguing about what to eat for breakfast. The original intention was lost in the bed sheets.

What's on your mind when you wake? If you aren't thinking what you want, change your mind before you get up.

THE BIG IDEA

Get up eagerly on your side.

What time of day do you get into your life?

What does it take for you to say, "OK, I'll do this day?" (Coffee and donuts? Perhaps a call from someone special?)

What do you think you are missing between the time you get up and the time you get into your life?

What was your first thought this morning when you awoke?

What might you have wanted your first thought to be?

What To Do On Purpose

Intention: To learn about living

TALKING ABOUT LIFE

Everyone has experienced those times in life when what was once thrilling has now become boring. All of a sudden you notice that your job has gone flat. The recollection of its exciting beginning is such a distant memory it's verging on folklore. You look at the past four years spent in psychotherapy and recognize that you no longer have movement in your life. Or you find yourself in church on Sunday morning wondering why you bothered to go.

"How do you get things to remain meaningful?" is the question. You want to go to church and have that experience make a real difference in your life. If not, why go at all? What creates special times when magic is made?

A predictable formula for creating extraordinary experiences is to get On Purpose in the moment. When you sit in church in your personality, nothing is quite right. The temperature is wrong; there are people around you who are distracting; the sermon is boring. However, just notice how everything is fine when you are there On Purpose. When you go deliberately. Everything provides food for inspiration, no matter how your personality would at other times judge it.

Have you noticed at work that you can have a day that is quite frustrating and, at another time, the same job can be quite fulfilling? It is clear that the job is constant in its content. However, your experience of it may change from day to day. The only place to look at what makes the difference is within yourself.

When you move through your life in your personality, Grenelda Thurman has the experience. And when you live your life On Purpose, your highest self is handling things.

When you show up at work On Purpose, you know this will not be a throw-away day. (How many days do you really want to discard in your life?) It will be a day that makes a difference. When you show up for counseling, On Purpose, you can be intentional about creating movement in your life. When you show up in church, On Purpose, you create for yourself the meaning.

STORY

A physician had a dream. He wanted to contribute to his profession and become known as a gentle and caring doctor. He never went to his office without being On Purpose. Everyday on the way to his office, he reminded himself of who he wanted to be. He left any concerns he had about his personal life at home. His medical practice flourished, and his patients loved him.

However, his home life was in serious jeopardy. He thought that he should be able to unwind at home, never having to be bothered. He puzzled over his relationships, believing that his family just didn't understand him. He didn't recognize that he had no interest in the affairs of his family. He somehow missed all of their important events. He was always too exhausted to participate with them about their problems, and he had almost no communication with anyone at home. In fact, they viewed him as a stranger. He never understood how important it was to live all the moments of his life On Purpose.

COMMENT

Everyone wants what they do in life to make a difference for themselves and for others. Before knowing about On Purpose, these happenings seem coincidental. When a person gets On Purpose, a difference is made.

THE BIG IDEA

Making a difference is the result of the action of a deliberate, On Purpose individual. The answer to the question, "What to do On Purpose?" is everything.

What have you forgotten to do On Purpose?

How will it make a difference if you do those forgotten things On Purpose?

What experience are you missing when you forget to be On Purpose?

How can you remember to get On Purpose for the experiences in your life?

Living On The Edge

Intention: To know what is

TALKING ABOUT LIFE

When you know *what is* about different issues in your life, you begin to make choices that are from a new premise. The new premise has you as the focus and what is best for you given the present circumstances. Knowing what is eliminates wishing for, hoping for, and thinking it will change.

What is carries no judgments that make you wrong, others wrong, or the situation wrong. What is simply is. You no longer feel some strange undercurrent inside. You actually feel relieved because you are no longer denying or lying to yourself. There is a freedom about knowing clearly what is and how you may choose for yourself knowing the truth.

Sometimes the choices are scary and overwhelming. You may begin to understand that you will want or need to do things that you had previously thought impossible. You may need to proceed without a predetermined plan. It may feel as if you are living on the edge. This is an experience of going ahead and making choices when you don't know the outcome. You are making decisions based on knowing what is about the present moment. You are no longer pretending about your life and how you have been manipulating it.

This may sound risky and, the truth is, it is risky. However, that is not all there is to this truth. When you live trying to manipulate what is you often experience disappointment. There is disappointment in yourself or others or the situation. You also may feel unfulfilled or dissatisfied with your life. Something is missing.

There really is nothing to do but to know what is and choose from there. You live one of two ways and both ways you live on the edge. When you manipulate your life by hoping and wishing, you are living with your eyes closed and you may fall off the edge of disappointment. When you choose from what is, you are living with your eyes wide open and have less potential for falling off the edge. You don't grieve for what you sacrificed or missed in life because you don't live with false expectations that keep you stuck. Your life expands because you grow as you see your life clearly.

STORY

A man spent twenty years being a loyal employee. He rejected several opportunities to expand his career with other companies, because he believed his loyalty would pay off. He hoped to be in the right place at the right time and someday his superiors would recognize and reward his efforts. He often wished he could land the right deal; then he would get ahead.

What he didn't want to know was this company never promoted from the inside. There was a company philosophy that major positions needed new blood. This man refused to know what is and follow his own best interest. He found himself in the position of being ten years behind in his career because he had his eyes closed living on the edge.

COMMENT

There is no safe way to live. Living itself brings risk and growth. When you live on the edge choosing what is, you are living with awareness about yourself.

THE BIG IDEA

Stay awake while you are living on the edge.

What choices have you made with your eyes open?

What are you still trying to manipulate to fit a particular outcome?

What choices have you made considering what is?

What were the results?

What do you need to presently look at from the perspective of what is?

Environmental Reorganization

Intention: To create your environment

TALKING ABOUT LIFE

Environment plays a more significant part in your efforts to live On Purpose than you previously may have thought. When holy people want to live a life of enlightenment, what they do is guard their environment. They create convents, monasteries, and ashrams to provide a secluded place of limited content. The smallest details are considered, so that they can live in a state of peace and harmony.

Of course, you probably don't want to run off to the Himalayas, to some hidden ashram so you can live On Purpose. However, you may want to live your life in peace and harmony. The manner in which you create your environment is extremely important to you.

Think of your environment as that place in which you spend a good portion of your time. It is the place that you have control of, to design and organize in a way that supports *you*. Take an inventory of the things that you love about your environment. Have you designed one room you love everything about, where every time you walk into it you feel supported and uplifted?

On the other hand, suppose in another room you have a picture that you hate hanging on the wall. Every time you see the picture, consciously

It's your space. Create it.

or unconsciously, you have a reaction of mild disgust. Maybe you have a closet in such a state that every time you open it you feel annoyed. How long does the annoyance stay with you?

How many items in your environment need your attention? What jarring thing do you continue to kick around because your deceased aunt gave it to you? What rooms would you love to start over on? Are you thinking, "Wonderful idea, but I can't hire a decorator"? Actually, you probably don't need or want someone else to design your place of peace and harmony.

What you need is to give it your time and attention and decide what would make you feel great every time you see it. It could be as simple as new drapes, a few plants, or the desk that you have always wanted. Think about what your favorite colors and designs are. Do you have any of them in your environment? Maybe you want soft colors to add some warmth. What are your dreams and how can you begin to incorporate them in your environment right now? Maybe you have always wanted a garden but you have no space. Be creative and get a plant box.

Another area to consider is who you are in relationship with. People with whom you live are a part of your environment. Wouldn't you want to have peace and harmony with them? Do you have unresolved issues hanging around that constantly create an undercurrent? How can you feel good about your environment with a cold war going on? You can recognize this problem if you hate to go home. You don't want to hate going home. You need a place that makes you feel good about who you are. Fending off a world of polluted skies and personal turmoil is enough to deal with. You don't want your environment to be any less than what you think of yourself or how you want to live.

Start with the little things. Clean out the

cupboards so every time you reach inside you feel good. Organize the garage so you aren't mad every time you want a hammer. Clean out the corner in the family room so you can create a space of your own. Wash the windows. And throw out anything you hate.

Reorganizing your environment can be fun because it will be about you. You will be making a statement about how you intend to live. A way that makes you want to be there all of the time. You will love the order you have and the way it makes you feel. You'll have more time because your attention won't be drawn to things you think you should be doing. You can get to those things you would love do, and nothing will be nagging at you.

You'll feel better about yourself because there won't be a hundred hidden undones waiting to upset you. You want your environment to reflect how you feel about yourself on the inside. Create your environment so that when the most important person walks in they experience lightness, and that most important person is you.

STORY

A young housewife has always dreamed of having a room of her own. The children have a playroom, the husband has a desk in the basement and a workplace, and the only space she can really call her own is her dresser drawers. She is seriously thinking about going back to school but does not see how this will be possible without some study space. She knows that unless she creates her life On Purpose her own goals will never materialize.

Fighting feelings of overindulgence and self-ishness that mothers often feel when they turn their attention to themselves, she decided that another corner of the basement could be cleared and set up quite comfortably. She enrolled her whole family in this project. When the space was complete, she realized that this was the very thing necessary for her to begin school. What seemed like an insurmountable task at the outset was just moderately difficult in reality.

COMMENT

Getting to know what is necessary and really wanting it in your life are the steps. Manifesting goals comes naturally out of the need, the want, and the knowing that you are a Purposed Being. Arrange your environment in a way that you and others know that you intend to live your life On Purpose.

THE BIG IDEA

It is important to create an environment that supports your living On Purpose.

What do you love about your environment?

How does your environment empower you?

How can you enhance your environment?

What does your environment say about you?

What would a stranger know about you by experiencing your environment?

Random Self—Purposed Self

Intention: To lead a Purposed life

TALKING ABOUT LIFE

Do you want a random life or a life that is On Purpose? How do you have any control over this issue? If your attention is not on your Purposed Self, your time and your space will be filled by accident, with anything that shows up. It becomes increasingly apparent that you have control over most of the content of your life; however, not all of it is under your control. When a hurricane blows you take cover, but how you spend your time under cover is your choice.

How do you make choices about content? If you want a life that makes a difference in the world, choose content that aligns with and supports your Purposed Self. If you do not choose the content you want in your life, what will show up is random content. Sometimes you will like it and sometimes you won't. Sometimes it will be related to your largest self, but often it isn't. It is simply random.

Just think about what happened when you finished a big project in your life. All of your children are finally out on their own. They were a big project for many years. What content showed up to fill the empty space created when they left? Obviously you were at choice about what to become involved in. If you didn't make

Whose side

are

you on?

that choice deliberately, any-old-thing probably showed up. This is truly random living, and living that way encourages your smallest self to take charge. Choose content that supports your Purposed Self, or let the Thurmans be in charge and watch what happens.

STORY

A young woman married. In her premarital state she was a competent professional with a large social circle and a few close and longtime friends. As she adjusted to her marital life she began to realize that in the act of marrying she had picked up all of her husband's content as her own. Where once she was an upwardly mobile professional, now she was mainly concerned with her husband's upward mobility. Her old friends were neglected because she had to meet her husband's social and business obligations. She found that less and less of her attention was taken up by her own content, and more space was devoted to her husband's content. This is not to say that the husband's content was inferior or somehow bad. It simply was not her content, content chosen by her to support her Purposed Self. Although the marital relationship added content to her life by its nature, she began to see that her balance was tipping from Purposed choices to random events.

COMMENT

Unless you take charge and fill your attention with content that supports your Purposed Self, content will show up randomly. Random content cannot be counted upon to call forth your Purposed Self.

THE BIG IDEA

The choice is yours. Choose your own content or take a chance on what comes along randomly.

What content keeps showing up that surprises you?

What content is in your life because you said so?

What content is in your life because someone else said so?

What content keeps you feeling stuck?

What content in your life is accidental?

What content are you now bored with?

When will you get rid of that content and what will you replace it with?

What content could you choose that would help you make a difference?

No Kleenex Days

Intention: To get present

TALKING ABOUT LIFE

To be alive in your life means living each moment of each day. And in the course of living you may notice that there are days you give up on. You literally quit living. Sometimes these days stretch into weeks and months. Something inside turns off, and you live the days as an unending stretch of moments to get through. As these thrown-away days lead one into another, you may notice that you are loving less and less of your life. The truth is that you don't want to throw away any of your moments or any of your days. All the days and all the moments count. You really want to live all of the moments of your life magnificently.

A kleenex day is a disposable day. It is a day that you have decided doesn't count in your life. Perhaps you wake up in a blue funk and give up on the day as you get out of bed. Maybe you don't even get out of bed. Perhaps something happens on the way to work and you check out. What happens when you check out of your own life is that something inside goes dead. You turn off inside, and from that moment on nothing counts with you. You are just getting through, without interest in the moments of your life.

Kleenex days become habits. We mistakenly think that it will be better if we go through the motions of our life not there. Some things facing us may seem difficult. We check out. We have to go through them anyway, but we try not to be present as they are happening. What does happen, then, is that we are not at choice about how we will be in the moment. We have turned off inside, and we cannot make choices about how we want to experience the day. Even as you lay sobbing on the bed or sit frustrated behind your desk, the world moves on. Opportunities knocking at your door go unheard and un- heeded.

STORY

A man started his work week with his usual Blue Monday attitude. He was at least a half hour late, complaining that he hadn't heard his alarm. He couldn't get anything accomplished until after the first coffee break and then it was slow going until noon. He did manage to get a half day in on Monday afternoon, but it wasn't anything to brag about.

During several evaluations he had been asked about his attitude, but he just couldn't shake it. Besides, he thought, people shouldn't be expected to do much on Monday, especially when they work hard the rest of the week.

He wasn't able to understand that every day counts. Every kleenex Monday he threw away added up.

COMMENT

Realizing that each day counts, each moment counts, enables you to live your own life as one of significance.

THE BIG IDEA

There are no kleenex days. Each day is a part of your whole life, a part of the process of your life's journey. Make sure that you are there as your life lives itself.

What days do you habitually throw away?

What interactions do you habitually throw away?

What have you thrown away that you would like to reclaim?

Why do you throw away days?

Control—Choice

Intention: To recognize choice

TALKING ABOUT LIFE

As you practice living your moments On Purpose, you will begin to notice how, when, and where your ego has control of you. Your ego is insidious enough, that when it catches on to the fact that you want to live On Purpose, it will want to take over. Your ego views life something like a game, and it wants to play and be the winner. In every situation it stands by with suggestions and judgments about how you should think, feel, or experience the content. It will remind you of previous consequences and encourage you to maintain control. When your ego is in control you have a predetermined idea of what behavior is best. You find yourself trying to control the present because of past experience. You miss out on the process of life because you are not at choice.

You know that your ego is masterfully subtle. The slightest variation in behavior can call forth your ego and its need to control. You will want to be on guard to make sure you are having an experience of the present moment. An experience that speaks to your living On Purpose.

You can never assume that the way you were once about any given situation will work twice. Your ego remembers everything you do with

Choosing

is easy.

Control

is hard.

great clarity. It remembers and evaluates. "This made me feel good or bad, this worked or not, this got me what I wanted." As your ego makes evaluations, it has little concern for growth, change, or fulfillment. Its major considerations are safety and control. It prefers the familiar without concern for your greatest self. It may be experiencing effort and struggle, but at least it is familiar and this is safe.

It is paradoxical that your ego wants to protect you from pain, and at the same time it causes you great pain. It causes you pain by keeping you stuck in emotions and thinking patterns that limit you and your experience of life. You may recognize that your ego wants to control you so that you only have what it considers good experiences. Your ego also may want to control others so that they do not challenge you. Your ego may want to control life circumstances so that you don't experience negative emotions.

The problem is that while your ego is in control, you are not at choice. When you are at choice, you never assume how it should be in reference to how it was or how you thought it might turn out. Remember that what worked before may not work a second time. You can only choose during the experience, not before.

You will want to choose positions about your experience that bring lightness to your life. Do you choose to believe that you are a victim of circumstance? Do you choose to believe that life isn't fair? Do you choose to believe that others exclude you? Do you choose to believe that you can't do the job? Do you choose to believe that you are right and they are wrong? Do you choose to believe that you have little value?

Find a position that lightens you up inside. You can confront your ego by deciding that you are going to let go of the evidence that your mind has collected to support its judgments. Choose to be the way that lightens the moment for you, and give up your expectations. If you take a position to get a particular outcome, you will be disappointed often. Choose in the moment to have lightness in your life.

STORY

A woman's ego tried to make sure she had a successful relationship. It had her believe that when she was a certain way, she could expect certain behavior from her significant other. Unfortunately, the more she tried to keep on top of things (troubles, emotions, jobs) the more resentful she became. She was resentful because her ego was not getting what it believed she deserved.

Eventually, it occurred to her that her ego was controlling how she was and what she did in her relationship to generate a specific outcome. When she realized she was giving with expectation, she recognized her ego's control. She began to look for ways she could choose to give of herself that had no expectations. She wanted to be in relationship just because that was what she wanted to do, nothing else. She wanted to give in the relationship just because that was what lightened up her life. She let go of her ego's expectations.

COMMENT

You can recognize ego control when you find yourself acting or reacting in a way that diminishes how you want to feel about yourself or others. You may feel perfectly justified about some position you have taken even though your position does not make you feel lighter. Be sure you notice this. Whenever you are struggling about yourself or others, it is a clue that your ego has a big investment in the outcome.

THE BIG IDEA

Those moments you can sincerely let go without expectation, you have surrendered ego control and you are at choice.

Identify times when you caught your ego wanting control.

Identify some times when you made a choice that didn't have any expectations.

How can you experience your choices about the moment more often?

Identify times you let go in a situation and you noticed that you lightened up on the inside.

There Are No Seams

Intention: *To connect your content*

TALKING ABOUT LIFE

When you consider the content of your life, do you believe some pieces are important and other pieces are less important? Do you review your day and feel as if it were filled with insignificant events? Who and what determines if the present content of your life is important?

When you review your life, you will notice that it has specific pieces of content that you remember and count as *your* life. You have relationships that you have declared as the most important relationships of your life. You have worked to achieve financial security that gives you the feeling of success. You have received an education that makes you proud. You have traveled and that has given you great pleasure. Or, maybe, you are waiting for some of these things to happen so you can count your life as significant. Maybe you believe that the content of your life just fills up the moments of your life. Maybe you continue to wait, not counting much of your life at all, just hoping that something important will happen.

There are no seams in your life. Cleaning house, gardening, vacationing, raising children, and landing the biggest business deal of your life are all of importance, because these events are a part of your life. Consider for a moment your whole life. What part would you eliminate? What could you do without and still be you? How would you have it be? What pieces of content keep showing up in your life that you refuse to do? Why did a piece of content show up in your life if it were not there for you to do? Whose life should it have shown up in?

Each piece of content affects every other piece of content. No seams is an idea to encourage you to view your life as a whole. The quality of the care of your children is affected by how you think and feel about yourself, your job, your whole life. There is a ripple effect. Everything flows into everything else. When you believe your life has seams, you believe you can get away with sloughing some of it off. No one will notice that you hate doing X, except you. You will never have to tell anyone about the horrible content of relationship Y, except that you know. And you try to separate it from the rest of your life.

If you are living a piece of content that you feel guilty about or that you think unimportant, stop your mind for a moment. Take a look at your life. Ask yourself, "Whose life am I living? Whose content is this?"

There are no seams in your life. Each piece of content has something in it for you. When you embrace your content fully, it moves you along in your personal journey, in your growth. Each piece of content affects the whole of your life.

You are the one that gives importance to the content of your life, and how you feel about your life is what gives the content its significance. Start viewing your life as a whole rather than in pieces and a shift will take place. You realize that what you are doing at the moment is the most important thing to be doing. You can trust the energy it has moment by moment. If it has energy, that is the content you should be doing. If it has no energy, move on to something else.

Give up the struggle, and do what is already in your life right now. Count it, and you will begin to see that life has no seams. You will realize that what you wanted to have the most is directly affected by what you absolutely refuse to do. So, live your life fully, count all your content as important, and continue to grow.

STORY

One woman had a very busy life. She had her own business that required her to be on the go. She also had small children who had many needs, and she felt responsible for her relationship with her spouse.

Many times she felt guilty and scattered about her responsibilities. She had difficulty giving her attention to the task she was doing. She complained that when she was working she felt as if she should be at home. When she was at home she felt she should be working. She couldn't focus on what was most important.

Ultimately, she learned that whatever she was doing was the most important thing to be doing. She loved her work and wanted to be successful. She loved her family and she wanted to participate with them. She realized that the only way to have it all was to be attentive to exactly what she was doing, when she was doing it. When she was with her family that was the most important place to be. When she was at work that was the most important place to be. No one place was more important than another because she loved it all. There were no seams. Everything counted for her.

COMMENT

When you love your life, you love your content. You trust that it is there for a purpose. You don't need to feel so much in control, for you believe that all is well because your content is the vehicle for your personal journey. You know that all of your life is important because there are no seams.

THE BIG IDEA

If it is in your life or if it has been in your life, it is extraordinarily important.

Where are the seams in your life?

What do you consider important?

What would it take for you to value your whole life?

What could you be doing that you are not doing?

What are the times you believe you got the wrong content and who might it have belonged to other than you?

What growth have you received from counting the content that is in your life?

See your life as a whole. What content did you try to skip?

What people arrived in your life that you rejected?

What events have happened that you pretended didn't happen?

Life Energy

Life Energies

TALKING ABOUT LIFE

Aliveness, Truth, and Workability are terms that describe three distinct, natural Life Energies. A natural Life Energy is an Energy that emanates from you and radiates around you. It is an Energy that you are born with that defines ways you process your life. You take in information and instantly it is refined to fit your particular Energy.

The idea of Energy is vague until you begin to examine yourself without judgments. Just ask yourself, "How do I do, naturally?" You already know that you try to *be* certain ways because you learned they were appropriate or you wanted to please someone else. Your survival instincts encourage you to be particular ways to get what you want and need. There are reasons you may deny the facts of your unique way of processing life. But when you get to the core of who you are, there is an Energy about you. One that makes you unique and special. It fits you. It feels like home to you.

You won't find any new ways to be when you learn whether you have the Energy of Aliveness, Truth, or Workability. You will simply learn that there is an Energy that describes you.

It describes your secret concerns about yourself. The ones that you always felt misunderstood about.

You will come to love yourself and your Energy because it is so basically who you want to be. You will learn special qualities about yourself and others. You will be able to communicate with others from your Life Energy. You will be empowered to love yourself because you are who you are, an Aliveness, Truth, or Workability Energy. You will unravel mysteries about the ones you love. You will know them more deeply because you won't need to judge them any longer. Each Life Energy has unique and identifying characteristics. By knowing those, you know amazing things about the people who have each type of Energy.

Aliveness

Aliveness Energy can be recognized by its excitement and visibility. People who have a predominant Aliveness Energy are intense and open. They stand out in the world because they are vibrant. Sometimes they are viewed as animated and stimulating. They believe in being lively and experiencing the world. Although they may enjoy moments of solitude, they often find themselves desiring the company of others, sometimes many others. They live their lives by trusting their experiences, and they are attracted to situations and people that will enhance their experience.

Identifying yourself as a person with the Energy of Aliveness means that you are fundamentally concerned with *experiencing*. Rarely do you back away from or say no to new experiences or new people. Often you are sought out for the joy of the experience you bring. You want your experience of living to be fun, to be enlivening; you move through the world expectantly and enthusiastically.

The Energy of Aliveness is expressive and noticeable. If you have the Energy of Aliveness, you draw other people into experience. You assist other people by encouraging them to experience their experience. Your enthusiastic and enlivening nature is a great gift to the world.

People who have the Energy of Aliveness love to share; you love to share yourself, and you love other people to share with you. You have a positive outlook on life and people are drawn to you to lighten up. The Energy of Aliveness enjoys a happy ending in life and looks for the silver lining. If you have the Energy of Aliveness, you value your relationships, old and new, and you don't burn your bridges behind you. You don't let people slip out of your life forever.

Truth

The Life Energy of Truth can be recognized by a soft sensitive manner. People who have a predominant Truth Energy seem serious and they are often quiet and introspective. They are sometimes viewed as analytical, interested in honor and justice, and they believe deeply in what they consider to be a good cause. They may find that they have a few intimate friends and other acquaintances. While they want your undivided attention and can give you undivided attention, frequently they are private and don't mind being alone. They look inside for guidance to make decisions and solve problems. They are attracted to those questions that speak to the meaning of life and their role in it.

Identifying yourself as having the Energy of Truth means you are fundamentally concerned with *knowing*. Rarely do you take anything at face value, because you want to know if there is a hidden agenda. With all of your senses, you are observant. You watch and listen beyond sight and hearing, because you know if something is in the air by what you sense. Your wanting to know includes understanding your own content.

Beyond that, you want to understand the fundamental causes of events. You know what is profound by its nature, so you live and move through the world respecting that which you regard as meaningful. More than likely you are intuitive, and you rely on your intuition to guide you. You are understanding, which enables you to know the larger picture.

Your profound nature is an exciting gift to the world. Wherever you are there is an Energy of meaning and sensitivity. Treasure your gift of Truth Energy, and you will find great fulfillment in being you.

Workability

When describing the Life Energy of Workability what first comes to mind is doing. Generally, Workability Energy has a productive nature about it. People with predominant Energy of Workability are seen as extraordinarily responsible; you can count on them. When a person with the Life Energy of Workability decides that something must be done, they will allow nothing to stand in the way of its accomplishment. If they commit to a project, it will get done. This does not necessarily mean that they will do all the work of it, but they know who to call and how to get things done.

If you have the Energy of Workability, you

may be described as even-tempered and companionable. You probably have a circle of good friends and are often considered indispensible to the life of the group. You do not mind being alone, but usually prefer a team approach.

Identifying yourself as having Workability Energy means that you are fundamentally concerned with *doing*. You understand what it takes to make dreams reality. From the simplest to the most complex project, you see the challenge of it. You have the ability to stay focused and organized. You are often the kind of person who makes to-do lists and actually uses them.

Productivity is a natural outcome of Workability Energy, and you have a singlemindedness of intention that is astounding. You remember to remember what it is that needs to be done. Your competence is recognized by those around you and you spend little time on what you might consider frivolous or irrelevant. You have a sense of appropriateness about yourself and your life that adds confidence to your overall orientation toward success.

Whatever it is, your Life Energy colors how you go through your life. Each way has a different way of being in the world.

Styles of Relating

As you learn more about yourself and your Life Energy, you will understand that you interact with people in a special way. Your Life Energy has a unique focus as it relates with other people. Others love your style of relating; they even seek you out for it.

Aliveness Energy. You relate by *engaging*. Your Aliveness Energy creates experiences with people. You talk with them because you are really interested in their lives. You love to interact with people, and you are able to engage with people everywhere—your friends, neighbors down the street, and strangers in the grocery line. There is a natural desire to laugh with people, to share with them.

Truth Energy. You relate by *attending*. Your Truth Energy enables you to know just what someone needs to make them feel special. Maybe you attend socially by surprising your guests with their favorite secret entertainment, dinner, or dessert. Maybe you attend by "accidentally" giving the perfect gift at the perfect moment. However you do, you are a master at giving attention.

Workability Energy. You relate to others by *being with* them. You are not concerned with where you go or what you do; you just want to be with people. It is not that you don't care about the content of the time, but what is most important to you is that you be together. This is not, as you know, a passive way to be. It is the creation of a marvelously warm and comfortable place of relating.

Ways of Getting Movement

When stuck in a situation or facing a dead-end, each Life Energy has a unique way of posturing that ultimately gets movement.

Aliveness Energy. When you are stuck and need to move, what you do is *start*. You know that to actually start, what you do is start—start—start. You start, until it is really started. That is why you start many things all the time. By starting, you get movement in your life. And you know that sometimes it takes many starts to actually get going.

Truth Energy. When you are stuck and need to move, what you do is *get willing*. Willing is extraordinary in that you prepare yourself for any outcome. Once you have looked at the worst scenario or the most challenging outcome that change could bring to see if you could live with it, you get willing and then the movement begins.

Workability Energy. What you do to get movement is to create an *intention*. An intention is a powerful singlemindedness, focused on a particular thing. There is an energy, a drive, that lives in the space of intention. Once you get intentional about something, you always remember to remember it. From this space you know that you could move mountains if it were necessary.

What You Get

Everyone is endowed with a special nature. Your Life Energy entitles you to a quality that facilitates your process of life. It seems to be your secret boost for being who you are. It's your built-in bonus.

Aliveness Energy. What you get is the *glory*. You get the attention and the applause. You are visible. You are remembered because of your zest. People want to be around you because often you are the center of attraction. Because of your visibility, people naturally give you the credit.

Truth Energy. What you get is *magic*. Magical

things enter your life, and magically things work out for you. The book you are supposed to read falls off the shelf onto you. You get the last motel room. You were not lost, but guided to the perfect place. It often seems as if your needs are fulfilled magically.

Workability Energy. What you get is the ability to *manifest* in the world. You know exactly what to do to get what you want. In fact, you know that manifestation begins with your wanting. You know what you want and you know that if you want it badly enough, you will do what it takes to get it.

Major Desire

Each Life Energy is guided by a unique desire about the quality of life. You have ideas about the necessary elements for a life of excellence.

Aliveness Energy. The major desire of your life is *no rules*. You know that everyone's experience is different, so you want no rules directing your life. You want to live your own experience, changing as you need to change. You feel that all people and all situations are different, so that any one set of rules cannot apply to all. People with the Energy of Aliveness believe that rules were meant to be broken.

Truth Energy. The major desire of your life is *no scarcity*. You believe you can have it all. You know that it is possible to have the perfect relationship, home, career, money, friends. Everywhere you see abundance on this planet; therefore, you believe in the possibility of everyone having it all.

Workability Energy. The major desire of your life is *no problems*. You know that problems can be avoided so you are always troubleshooting three miles down the road. You know that getting what you want is at risk when problems are around.

Tone

Each Life Energy has a special inflection that identifies its uniqueness. Each one has a noticeable manner, a certain style. You will reflect yours as the spirit you bring to life, the manner in which you experience your life, your mode of being, or your particular mood.

Aliveness Energy. Your tone is *spontaneous*. You often make decisions about what you will do moment to moment. You don't want your plans set in concrete, so you sometimes change your mind midstream. This spontaneity helps you and those around you experience a zest for living the moment, at the moment.

Truth Energy. Your tone is *acceptance*. With little hesitation, you accept others the way they are. You watch, guarding against expectations. You extend your ability of acceptance to life situations. Your motivation seems to be to make others and their situations OK by accepting them.

Workability Energy. Your tone is *reliability*. When you commit to a job, no reminders or motivation are needed because you are absolutely responsible. If you say you will do it, no matter what content shows up, you will.

Manner

Aliveness Energy. Your manner is *exciting*. When you arrive, people notice, because there is always something unexpected in you. You generate enthusiasm and energy around you. Having this manner brings life to the situation.

Truth Energy. The manner you have is *easy*. You adapt yourself to many situations without disturbance. You give others a lot of space and take up little space for yourself. Having this manner makes you easy to be around.

Workability Energy. The manner you establish is *safe*. "Don't worry, I'll handle it," is a frequent response. Because of the desire to have no problems, you are always creating the overall effect of safety. People come to expect and rely upon the space of safety that you create.

STORY

Once a person with Aliveness Life Energy went for Thanksgiving to the home of a family where every member had the Life Energy of Workability. At the end of the day she knew that the tone of the entire family was different than her own. She was used to the Energy of Aliveness; lots of starts, and lots of sharing in loud interactive conversation. What she had experienced was a day with perfect Workability Energy; lots of intention, great organization, team work, and companionable enjoyment of each other's company.

You are able to recognize yourself as a person with the Life Energy of Aliveness, Truth, or Workability. You embrace the affinities; you recognize the strangeness. It is wonderful to identify your Life Energy because it liberates you from the world of judgments about yourself. If you have the Energy of Aliveness, you might have said, "I start so many things. I always want to follow through, but I just can't seem to do it. I'm a failure." Now you know that that is how Aliveness Energy gets movement.

As you are able to recognize your predominant Life Energy, you may also recognize the Energy you need. If you need Aliveness Energy you might say, "I just don't know how to start things. There is nothing wrong here. This is just how I am." From personality you might have said, "I am so awkward. I can't start things. I feel so inadequate about it all."

You are able to identify your Life Energy, and by doing so, you will be able to lighten up about your life, about how you do. Because how you do is right. How you do is great. This is your life, and how you do is about your Life Energy.

THE BIG IDEA

Knowing your Life Energy lets you look at your life nonjudgmentally. It lets you lighten up.

Life Energy has no hierarchy. The most important thing is to recognize and accept how you are. It could be that you recognize a predominate Energy and you can't really understand another. You may notice that you have some of the qualities of all three Life Energies, yet one Energy describes your innermost secrets. You may think you are basically one Energy; however, you know a lot about a second one. It's not as important to label yourself as to understand something natural about yourself. Take time to review and see where you feel most at home.

What Life Energy is most familiar to you?

What Life Energy have you thought you would like to be more like?

What Life Energy irritates you the most?

What Life Energy do you believe you are?

What Life Energy are you least familiar with?

Who Are My People?

Intention: To love your people

TALKING ABOUT LIFE

When you want to live On Purpose, you need to lighten up by dropping your judgments about yourself and others. Knowing about Life Energy enables you to understand something about others without analyzing them. You can see them as interesting instead of wrong. They are different than what you understand, but that does not mean you can't find a way to relate to them. You don't want to change yourself to fit their judgments, and you don't want them to change to fit yours.

You could be trying to model changes you think you need after someone who has a Life Energy that you know nothing about. Or maybe you have convinced them they should be more like you, causing them to feel inadequate about who they are naturally and what they are capable of giving spontaneously in life.

Your Life Energy leaves your signature wherever you are. It is the Energy that says you are unique and how you are counts. Aliveness Energy brings excitement, Truth Energy brings understanding, and Workability Energy brings cooperation to this planet.

You get more of yourself when you realize that, and that there is nothing wrong with you or the people in your life. Maybe they don't need to get something fixed. It could be that they fundamentally experience life with an Energy that you are unfamiliar with. Wouldn't it be interesting to get to know something about an Energy that you have avoided until now?

When you are not judging other people, you have more space to find out what is really going on with them. Look at them with the idea that you want to know who they are. What is their Energy about? Is it different than yours? Is it your lowest Energy? Does their Energy make them wrong or does it make them unique?

Knowing someone's Life Energy could enable you to rewrite your history with them. You realize they were not doing something to you. They react to the experience of life differently than you do. It enables you to take their responses impersonally. They were responding from their Energy, which is the best way they know how.

Learn about Life Energy to understand yourself and others without judgments. Be yourself—let them be themselves. There is no right way to be. Your way is the best way to be, as is their way the best way to be. Ultimately, you want to develop those Energies that you find missing. You want to have it all, and someone whose Life Energy is your low Energy can be a great teacher for you. Discover what they have, and you discover something about yourself.

STORY

A young man whose Life Energy was Aliveness experienced whatever he was doing with intensity. His friendships were as intense as his passion for sports. He played hard, studied hard, and generated energy around him. He was never quiet, and he loved to share everything. He was constantly being grounded for inappropriate behavior, like breaking the rules, and so on.

Both of his parents had Truth Life Energy. They enjoyed and needed a quiet harmonious atmosphere. Their son seemed disrespectful of their need for privacy with his constant demands and interruptions. They might come home to a house full of strangers who just dropped in to speak with their son. Also, it seemed as if he purposefully broke the rules they agreed upon. Sometimes, they believed he was irresponsible, and they were beside themselves about what to do with him.

When they discovered that his Life Energy was the Energy that they knew the least about, they began to question who this child really was. Could it be that their evaluation of him wasn't true?

How could they begin to know him? They decided to reserve their judgments about him for a few days. They began to experience their son's Energy as interesting. They noticed the way he was with renewed curiosity. They saw his need for engaging with others. They realized he was not barging in to upset them. He just loved to be a part of the action. He had a great zest for experiencing.

They also began to learn something about themselves. They saw their hesitancy to start, their reluctance to engage with strangers, and their tendency to be so serious.

COMMENT

If you want to learn more about someone, learn about their Life Energy. You will have fewer judgments about how they are, which creates more space for them to be around you. Learn about your own Life Energy and you will have more space to be yourself. You will get at home with the way you are. Your self-esteem will flourish, which will enhance the quality of your life.

THE BIG IDEA

Knowledge of Life Energy will empower you to experience your people with fewer judgments. They will have space to be how they are. Remember, "Oh, that's how they do."

What is your Life Energy?

What Life Energy do you have the least of?

What Life Energy do the members of your family have?

What Life Energy did your caretakers have as you were growing up?

Who would you like to find out more about?

Who do you have difficulty understanding?

What fascinates you about someone close to you?

Does someone close to you have a Life Energy that you have the least of?

What misunderstandings does that cause, if any?

What additions does it bring to your life, if any?

What Life Energy would you like to develop more of?

What judgments about yourself are you able to give up?

What judgments about someone else are you able to give up?

Don't

take

them

personally.

Living On Purpose

The Other

TALKING ABOUT LIFE

If you could look into the future and preview the final chapter of your life, what would you want to see? Wouldn't it be your choice to see yourself loving the people in your life? Would immediate problems be so significant? Would you want to have forgiven any betrayals? Would you or anyone *want* to see themself spending their last week frustrated and irritated in all their relationships?

Isn't it true that right now you want to love your families, significant others, your friends and neighbors? Before it is the end? Isn't it a fact that you would love them, unconditionally, if they would just behave? You find yourself starting out, willing, with the best of intentions with them, and you've got something great going. Suddenly, they do something that so disturbs you that you feel as if you are in relationship to a stranger. They do that one thing that turns you off. Perhaps you didn't understand their last comment or you took it personally. Maybe you tried to do them a favor, and you felt that they trashed your efforts. What could possibly be happening, when all you wanted to do was to love them?

They have just become the other to you. The

person whom you don't understand at all. The one that drives you crazy. The one that, you are sure, there is no hope for. After all, you are a good judge of character and this other doesn't fit any category you know about. And then they expect you to be close to them, after they just ruined your life with their last statement. You know you don't ask for much from them, but you would like some respect.

A big problem is that this may be describing someone you plan to live your life with. It could be your children or your significant other. There is a big problem sharing your life with someone who consistently becomes a stranger. You never know for sure just what they might do or say that will turn your life upside down.

The following are just a few of the reasons why your intimate people sometimes become strangers to you.

Because you misunderstood their communication.

Maybe they were being intimate with you and you took it lightly.

Because they misunderstood your communication to them.

Maybe they didn't realize you were trying to help rather than control their life.

Because they rarely take your life problems seriously.

It is true you are happy most of the time, but sometimes you also have trouble.

Because you are not willing for them to be certain ways with you.

Maybe the one way you love to be, they hate to be.

Because they will not start anything.
They have great ideas about projects but they never get started. You have to start conversations, entertainment, even sex.

Because they want you to want things you do not want.
Maybe they think they know what things would enhance your life and you have no desire to have those things or you think those things are frivolous.

Because they hurt your feelings by not attending to you.
Maybe they don't know how.

Because you thought you did know them.
Did you actually know them, or did you assume that they should look like what you want them to look like in relationship?

Because the way they are is how you figured out not to be.
Certain behaviors work for you, and their behavior does not remotely fit what works for you.

Because you have judgments about them.
They are too loud, too boring.

Because you have judgments about you.
You should be more outgoing like they are, except you notice you would rather be alone.

Because you think they have judgments about you.
You think that they trash your desire to have organization.

Because you think they think you have judgments about them.
You think they believe that you want them to

stop having fun, when you love their enthusiasm.

Because what moves you, stops them.
Special things excite you and they are the very things that they hate.

Because what moves them, stops you.
They have special things that excite them and they are the very things you hate.

Because you think if you are not on guard, they will bring out the worst in you.
You have figured out what makes you feel great and they somehow trash your experience.

Because the way they are is the thing inside of you that is never handled.
The theory of mirroring tells us that what we see that is disturbing in others is the same thing that disturbs us about ourselves.

This list begins to give you a clue that something significant is happening when someone we love turns into the other. Often what is happening is that they are being the way they are naturally, and it seems most unnatural to you. The more you can recognize your own predominate Life Energy, the more you can recognize the Energy of the people in your relationships. Maybe you absolutely identify with one Energy, and you haven't the vaguest idea about another Energy. If you are married to someone with a Life Energy you don't recognize, they will, at times, become the other to you. The manner that they are perfectly at home with may be the very thing that you are wanting changed.

Give up your efforts to judge or to analyze and correct the natural Energy of someone you love. If you are not familiar with their Life Energy, perhaps you need to learn more about it. Forgive the ones you love for missed communications, forget their past faux pas. Did they really mean it, or did you receive it differently than they meant it?

When you become interested in someone whose Energy is different than yours, it is an opportunity to begin identifying and understanding a fundamental source of your own issues. If you see your other as frustrating and peculiar, what might you be missing? What can another Energy teach you that would be valuable for you to know? Take a second glance and see if they are really trying to do something *to* you. More often than not they could just be expressing their own Life Energy and they would be pleased if you appreciated it.

If you have low Workability Energy, maybe you aren't able to produce as much as you would like. If you have low Aliveness Energy, maybe you have a hard time getting started. If you have a low Truth Energy maybe you have trouble being intimate with others. Knowing about Life Energy gives you a clue as to where you could focus to glean information about qualities you have felt lacking.

STORY

. A woman whose Life Energy was Workability was providing childcare for her friend, who had low Workability Energy. The mother returned for her daughter early one afternoon, only to find the child napping. She told the woman how surprised she was to find her daughter asleep, because she never took naps. The woman said she hadn't had any trouble getting the young girl to sleep.

The friend asked what her secret was. The

woman with Workability Energy looked at her oddly and said, "Well, it was nap period."

"Nap period?" asked the mother.

The woman explained that the children had a reading period, a play period, a dance period, and a lunch period. After lunch period, they had nap period, and that was why the young girl was sleeping.

The friend was amazed. She couldn't believe children would nap just because it was nap period. But the woman assured her the children knew when nap period came, and they even asked about it if they were off schedule. How wonderful, her friend thought, to have the children so organized and cooperative.

COMMENT

Every Life Energy is special. If you are unfamiliar with one, take time to notice it. It could explain what you have considered to be problem areas in your life.

First, love who you are naturally. Second, see if you want to experience more of what you don't have. Third, get into a relationship with someone whose Life Energy is what you have the least of and see what you can learn from them.

THE BIG IDEA

When you are are not judging someone else for how they are, they become less of the other and more of your teacher. You can rewrite your history with them; you can stop taking them personally.

Who is the other in your relationships?

How does their Energy feel to you?

What have you always tried to get them to understand that they never understand?

What is one thing that you have always taken personally that you now see was the other just being natural?

What do you now appreciate about the other that you faulted them for before?

What fascinates you about the others in your life?

What is your lowest Life Energy?

What do you need to know about it?

Love Me—Love Me Not

Intention: To love loving who you love

TALKING ABOUT LIFE

Aliveness

Have you found yourself in love with a person with Aliveness Energy? If so there are a few things you probably would like to know. Questions you might ask yourself are why you are so attracted to them and why you can't leave them alone. It's because they know how to keep you fascinated, and they plan to be the center of your thoughts. Do not be alarmed and do not plan to disappear. They may seem distracted at times but they purposefully keep you interested enough that you won't want to go far away.

It's their charisma that keeps you captivated even if you are frustrated with them. And often they do frustrate you because you can never pin them down. They seem to get so involved with the moments of their living, it looks like they have an out-of-sight, out-of-mind manner. (No, they haven't forgotten you. It's just that they stopped to say hello to someone and the person needed a friend to talk with. People with Aliveness Energy are often the friend, and after all, it was a crisis.)

Do not assume who or what should be important to them because that would drive them crazy. They could create a drama that you might never forget. Their lives are often dramatic because they have an animated style, one that makes their experience visible. Their experience changes from moment to moment and they tend to act it out. If they have caused a scene, don't worry; they know how to make it right.

They cannot tolerate your not speaking for any reason. It doesn't matter too much if you aren't interested. They will continue to start, start, start with you until you respond. Actually, they are extraordinarily interested in you and your problems. Just talk to them and they will make it worth your while. No matter how bad you feel, they can charm you into feeling great about yourself.

When they love you they are on your side. Everyone will be convinced you're wonderful, maybe to your surprise. If you suddenly feel popular and are receiving more invitations than you ever had before, remember how it happened. It's because someone with Aliveness Energy loves you and knows that everyone else will too.

However don't be possessive. Pay attention and you will see that they are genuinely interested in people, people, and more people. They are fascinated with all of the details of people and their lives. They keep in touch with everyone, and are sincerely concerned about their lives. And they never get rid of people. They are likely, after a ten-year absence, to contact an old love and want to know everything that has happened in the interim. Which means, of course, they will never get rid of you and they will always be interested in your life.

Also you must know that they do not live quiet secluded lives. Without ever trying, they draw attention to whatever they are doing and they want you to participate. They truly want you to have a great time in your life and they will be flexible to insure that you do. People with Aliveness Energy have enormous good-will. They would like nothing more than for everyone, especially you, to be happy and smiling inside.

Amazingly, they produce evidence of your magnificence even when you are sure you have failed. Listen to this person you love. They are positive you, and your life, is worth loving no matter what you think; and they will lovingly show you how.

They help you fully experience life, whatever that will mean. One moment you will be pressed to make a scene, followed with their applause. If you want to get the gist of experience you must look to the moment. Whatever is in the moment is what a person with Aliveness Energy is experiencing. They love life, the moments of it, the people in it, the experience of it. You will definitely have a great loving time.

Workability

The day you fall in love with a person with Workability Energy will certainly be your lucky day. You always attributed their good fortune to luck, and now you love one of them. If they think you are special, their good luck will surely be yours.

They may seem bossy at times but look again. They just know what they want, and they are determined to have it. And if they love you they will want you to have what you want. You must be prepared because they never want small. They know more about want than you could dream possible.

Make no mistake, wanting is not all they do. It may seem as if they want to control you but they know when your life is upside down, and they just want to help set it right. In your chaos they will find order, and organize your life to fit your style. While you are wondering what has happened, they are enrolling you in yet another project that will enhance the productivity of your life. And they will do it in a way that you can hardly fault, because you really will have more and better in your life.

Thanks to the person you love who has Work-ability Energy, your life is now on the upswing. You may be frustrated with the new schedule in your life but you are finally going places that you always dreamed of going. If you didn't dream of getting ahead, you had better start because when they discover your dreams they will manifest them for you.

They have a can-do nature and will rarely tolerate you saying it can't be done. You are in for a surprise if you have a few favorite problems. They can banish problems with a single word. If you continue to indulge you may end up feeling incompetent, for they want you to have a world void of problems.

They know about success, and they really pull it off. They are true to you and are committed to your success. When they love you they will want you to be safe and content. But please don't leave them out. They want to do what you want to do. They sometimes can be demanding but when they are it is for a good reason. After all, they have proof that they know what's best.

If you are bothered about their constant attention to details, you may want to exercise patience. Not only do they know what is best, they also know what is appropriate. Do not take it personally if they reprimand you for having no class. In every situation they believe they know what works and, foremost, they believe you must be appropriate. You may need to gently remind them that what is appropriate for them may not be appropriate for you.

In all of their stubbornness they can be quite

fluid, if you can change their mind. But they will try to divert you. Therefore you must persist with your point of view. Loving a person with Workability Energy will enhance your life. They will be great companions and hold you in high esteem. Even when they are angry with you, you can count on them to slay your dragons. It will be a powerful life loving one of them. And if they become committed they will be yours forever.

Truth

If you find yourself wondering who is this secretive person that haunts you, you may be falling in love with someone who has Truth Energy. Even though they seem secretive they will expect to know everything about you, and eventually they will. Pay attention if they are constantly on your mind; they have decided that you will not forget them. And if you look closely, you will discover that they deliberately move mountains to insure that they remain important to you.

However be informed that the more you do to enchant them the more elusive their affection seems. Realize it is their love of intimacy that keeps you forever trying to discover who they really are. It would be unwise to give up your efforts if you want a solid love who adores you.

Don't get worried yet. If you need attention, they are at your beck and call. They will provide your favorite things before you even mention them. And they will send you flowers and other perfect gifts for no reason at all; except, of course, to win your everlasting love and undying affection.

While they will rivet their attention on you, they will also demand their privacy. It's not that they are hiding something, it's just their sensitivity. If they have allowed you in their life, you will see that they are sensitive to everything, especially to you.

Their interest in you is extraordinary. They will be your biggest cheerleader and support your secret desires. If you have ambitions, they will convince you that the impossible can be done as they support you in walking that extra mile. They have an ability to make you feel more special than you have ever felt. They know and understand those issues about you that would make someone else flinch. It's because they know how to forgive you, and once you have been honest with them, they see your perfection all over again.

They will hardly ever hold a grudge against you but you must beware. If you can get close enough to know their deepest secrets, they will expect you to guard those secrets in your heart. And if you should betray their most intimate details, they probably will fade off into the sunset and you will be a distant memory.

Go ahead and love a person with Truth Energy if you dare. They can charm your friends and relatives, and be impressive with your boss. But you must remember, they hate a facade and they need an environment where truth and honesty prevail. Don't let their seriousness put you off. They are honestly looking for the meaning. Their analytical nature searches for the bottom line. Somehow they intuitively know just what is needed to bring you happiness.

They are gentle loving people who feel close to the earth. Don't let their soft quiet nature intimidate you; they are just listening to words you can't hear. If you want someone who is easy to be around, love your person with Truth Energy with all your heart. They are loyal and trusting, with a certain innocence. You may at times need to protect them from their own naivete.

Loving a person with this Energy will certainly be profound. When you capture their attention, your life will have new meaning. Suddenly you will realize that your life does matter more than you dared dream possible.

STORY

Once upon a time a man was looking for a love. He met an exciting woman who seemed to be extraordinarily interested in his life. She was curious about the people he interacted with and loved to talk with him about them.

Her passion for living was infectious. She could always find the bright side and make him feel great even when he thought life was dismal. He often wondered if she ever had any problems because she was always positive and enthusiastic. Everywhere they went together, she seemed to leave little sparkles of zest behind her. Being with her he noticed just how much he was enjoying his life.

He was fascinated with her ability to attract attention, but sometimes irritated by it, too. He could never seem to pin her down. Her outgoing nature made him wonder if he was significantly important to her. However whenever she was with him, it seemed as if he was her one and only interest. It was a paradox to him. No one had ever been so obsessively interested and enthusiastic about him yet so evasive.

A close friend introduced him to another woman. Immediately he developed a new interest. This woman seemed stable and secure. She was ambitious and successful. He dated her a few times and noticed how companionable she was. Whatever he wanted to do was really fine with her. She enjoyed being with him and loved to help him plan his weekly schedule. He even noticed his sales were improving; it did make him wonder about her. She often impressed him with her knowledge of what he needed to improve his lifestyle.

One thing that did bother him was her persistence. She knew in advance what needed to be handled and she rarely deviated from her goal. She refused to forget responsibility and throw caution to the wind. If she had her mind made up that a task had to be completed before she ran off to relax, nothing he did could change her mind.

Anyway, his brother had introduced him to another woman. This woman was a puzzle. He wasn't sure he liked her when he first met her. She was serious and secretive, but she quickly knew things about him that no one else knew. When they were together she riveted her attention on him. Finally he felt understood. She was fond of quiet evenings of intimate conversation and somehow she knew what would please him. This woman inspired him to be more open. He realized she had him thinking and doing things that meant more to him.

While they rarely made elaborate plans, their times always magically worked out. They would just get together and somehow they did the perfect thing. If he was under pressure and busy, she was easy to be around. She could make herself invisible while still being available.

It might have been perfect for him except this woman was starkly honest. Her honesty made him uncomfortable. She always expected him to say what was true, no matter what.

You can draw any conclusion to this story. The point will be the same. Love the love that finds you, because there is no one better.

You rarely can solve relationship problems by changing relationships. If you look for disappointments, you can usually find them. If you misunderstand someone you love, it doesn't mean they need to change. It is amazing how lovable people can be when you focus on what is lovable about them.

THE BIG IDEA

When you love someone, love their uniqueness.

What is unique about the person you love?

What do you understand about them that you didn't understand before?

What do you need to tell them about why you love them?

What difference would it make to them?

What difference would it make to you?

Rewriting Your Personal History

Intention: To love your past

TALKING ABOUT LIFE

A real nuisance of childhood is the incessant evaluations. Your educational years were beset with assessments, with everything from intelligence to social conduct being graded. If you had many check marks by "needs improvement," you are likely to be harboring some old issues.

To add to your troubles, your guardians had ideas of how you should turn out. If you were good, did you get the credit? And if you were different, were you labeled the black sheep? What social opinions convinced you that you are deficient? When you can look beyond these judgments, there is a future for your healing and success.

You can begin the process by determining what your family composition is in terms of Life Energy. What Energy did your parents have and was it compatible with your Energy? As a child, was it difficult for you to give attention to your parents or siblings? Were you always complaining that you were misunderstood in school? Maybe you wanted to cooperate, but you always managed to be breaking some rule. Did you feel as if no one appreciated your help or wanted your

Take

another

look.

companionship?

To a child some of these issues can loom large. Were you a child who took differences personally? In your efforts to please, maybe you made decisions about yourself and your family that had little to do with the facts; like times you wanted to get some peace and quiet and your siblings called you a sissy, so therefore you grew up feeling powerless.

Your parents might have been as perplexed about you as you were about them. Wouldn't it be freeing to see that the trouble was probably about differences in Energy? A child with Aliveness Energy probably wasn't really being nosey, just *interested*. Maybe another child with Truth Energy was *introspective*, not shy and withdrawn. And children who have Workability Energy, of course, might have been real *organizers*, instead of bossy and stubborn.

Knowing about your Life Energy and how it affected you in the past can help you rewrite your history. You can begin to give up your judgments about your family, school, and other institutions. Maybe they weren't doing anything *to* you. It could be as simple as, "That's just how they do."

Your family is the only family you have. Wouldn't you like to accept your family and have them accept you? Families are important people to make peace with because that's like making peace with part of you. You can look anew at your family. See them as people you are curious about, who have different or the same Life Energy. Get to know how they are, what is important to them, what they dislike, what they love.

Your history says a lot about you. It has given you the opportunity to turn out. But history is not destiny. Give up your judgments and you can love yourself, love your family, love your history.

STORY

A woman discovered that she had Truth Life Energy. When she began to look at her history she made some interesting discoveries. She had always felt a little at odds with her family. When she attended reunions, she continually felt as if she was missing something. The things that were important to other family members, she considered insignificant. She wanted to discuss topics that they considered to be too serious. They believed that she found life's content too meaningful, and they thought she never wanted to have any fun.

There was a problem of teasing. She never saw the humor in their constant funny remarks, and she believed that they had little consideration for other's feelings. She took their remarks seriously.

But she loved to have family gatherings. She knew how to attend to people and make them feel special. However, most family members arrived late, if at all, and it was a constant frustration to her. She took their behavior personally, believing they didn't like her.

When this woman examined the Energies of her family she saw something. She was the only one with Truth Energy. Most of her siblings had Aliveness Energy and the rest had Workability Energy. What was important to her was how they had learned not to be. What was important to them she thought was frivolous.

She stopped judging them. She started to pay attention to how they did, rather than how they did to her. She was in the process of rewriting her history.

COMMENT

Look at your family. Could what you thought were irreconcilable differences be differences in Life Energy? It is to your benefit to love your past and the people in your past.

THE BIG IDEA

History is not destiny. Re-view it.

What judgments about yourself can you give up by understanding your family's Life Energy?

What judgments about your family members can you give up by understanding their Life Energy?

What would you now like to know about your family that you refused to consider before?

What areas, other than family, did you have difficulty interacting in?

What content areas of your life do you want to rewrite?

Manage Your Body

Intention: To understand your vehicle

TALKING ABOUT LIFE

When you decide that you are up to something in your life and you want to do something about it, suddenly thoughts about your body become significant. You may experience that you don't have the energy you need, or the look you need, or you don't feel as good as you would like in order to express yourself in the world. Your mind might convince you that your body can't get the job done for various reasons.

You already know that you are not your body, and you have worked to identify yourself in other ways. You may be experiencing a need to manage your body for reasons other than ego gratification. Maybe you have decided that your health is your present focus and you need to change the way you eat, or you may need to consider giving up addictive habits. Perhaps you have decided that you need an exercise program to help you maintain a certain energy level. Whatever your reasons for deciding to turn your attention to your physical vehicle, now you must decide what really makes the difference about your body.

You must decide to manage your body for some other reason than what your ego makes up. The shift comes by first recognizing what is, by not judging the present circumstances, and by

This is the only body you have.

It's best to love it.

calling forth your Purposed Self to direct you toward the necessary changes. Your major job in managing your body is to continue to do all the things that lighten you up about it. Just simply follow those ideas and thoughts that make you feel light. Does it really make you feel light to continue to be sedentary? Does it really make you feel light to carry around those extra twenty pounds? Does it really make you feel light to hang onto your addictions? Just ask yourself these questions each time you need to make a decision about managing your body and continue to choose what lightens you up. When you want to express your essence and have the world relate to *you* and not your vehicle, you will decide to manage your body.

STORY

A woman had a problem about being overweight. This caused her to withdraw from life. Her once lucrative business was suffering because she hated to meet new people. She was sure that they found her weight annoying. Her previously active social life was deteriorating because she often was too embarrassed to accept invitations. She told herself it was because she didn't have the right wardrobe or that she was too busy.

She constantly condemned herself, believing that she was her body. The problem accelerated, as she told herself that she had no will power, she was unorganized, and, besides, she should be ashamed of herself. Everyone knew, she thought, overweight is an example of no control.

One day she began to realize that her problem of excessive weight could not be solved from her mind. Her mind had already gotten her off and

on to a hundred diets, and she still was overweight. She decided to buy clothes that fit rather
than waiting for the weight to come off. She
started saying yes to social invitations. Also, she
stopped assuming that others had judgments
about her. She had opportunities every day to
decide what she wanted to do about her weight.

COMMENT

You are not your body. You are just in charge
of managing your body. Your body is only an issue if it is an issue.

THE BIG IDEA

Your body is simply your vehicle to
express all that you want to be.

What thoughts do you have about your body?

How do your thoughts about your body empower you?

How do your thoughts about your body limit you?

How have you tried to change your body?

What do you choose to do today, considering your body as your vehicle?

When was a time you loved your body as your vehicle? Why?

Who are you when you don't believe you are your body?

What difference will it make in your life to accept that *you* are not your body?

Handle Your Emotions

Intention: To master emotions

TALKING ABOUT LIFE

Emotions can be one of your most formidable challenges when you decide that you want to live your life On Purpose. It would be easy to be generous, compassionate, and understanding, if you were never caught off guard by crippling emotions. Fortunately there are times that you can look at your emotions objectively and discover interesting choices about how you want to be.

The power of emotions and their effect must never be taken lightly. How many times have you found yourself thinking you have dealt with a traumatic situation only to find yourself suddenly paralyzed by the emotional memory of that once forgotten event. You realize that you can no longer remember the details of the trauma but the emotion is uncomfortably familiar. There is content that has made you wonder how you could be so devastated by an issue that seemed so irrelevant. Your spouse removed a piece of lint off your jacket and you found yourself immobilized with anger.

Also there are times that you are determined to react differently to the same piece of content. But the same old argument begins. You say A, they say B, then you say C, so they say D. By the time you get through the alphabet, you have

If you want

to be

loved,

be

lovable.

Living On Purpose

stormed out not speaking once again. Then you make up, with promises that it will never happen again, until the next alphabetical encounter of course.

It's not even that you don't have a valid point. Maybe you are thoroughly justified in your anger or disappointment. But whose day is thrown away? What important work didn't get accomplished? Who can't sleep nights? How far is the setback from your personal goals?

And if it gets really awful you begin to believe you are an ogre. You think that you are your emotional behavior and you agree that you are a wimp, or a witch, or whatever you have been accused of being in your most recent emotional encounter.

Suddenly you are on a familiar downward spiral that ends up with you having only a vague recall of what living On Purpose meant to you. You can't remember that you felt powerful or that your life had meaning and Purpose. You begin to wonder if you are up to making a difference because you can't even seem to settle it with your own people.

To prevent your spiral downward, you want to differentiate between emotions and feelings. Emotions stem from an undercurrent of hidden agendas. They are fed by your persistent denial of what is true for you. Your efforts to behave in a way you truly are not, to do things you do not choose to do, or to give with expectations will lead you down a path toward confronting your out-of-control emotions.

You could be flirting with trouble if you depend on your emotions to guide you or to help you make decisions. Decisions that you make that are based on anger, frustration, infatuation, or other emotions are not reliable. Tomorrow you may not be angry or infatuated, and here you are stuck with some inapplicable decision that you have made.

Your emotions create disturbance and imbalance, because they are so changeable. It is giving a lot of control to someone else if you have decided that their morning call or their particular mood can emotionally influence your day. You can end up living your day experiencing their emotion.

Feelings, on the other hand, can add color to your life and tell you a lot about yourself. You can separate feelings from emotions by recognizing the genesis of them. The genesis of feelings is you, and the genesis of emotions is something or someone else. Feelings have an energy that originates internally that may or may not have to do with an external experience.

You experience loving from the inside and then you notice that love on the outside finds you. If you find yourself unexpectedly sad or frustrated, it may be something inside that needs to come out. Feelings do not paralyze you because you are still at choice. There is a little you sitting on your shoulder watching, helping you decide about your feelings from moment to moment. It asks you how long you want to be sad or how many days you are going to be angry?

While feelings will keep you in touch with your experience of living, you may want to transform your emotional drama. If you want to change this situation, you must catch yourself before you are in the middle of your act. Watch to see what is coming when you think particular thoughts. If you notice you are getting unsettled, you may want to decide what you are going to do differently. You may want to start with Z rather than A. Maybe you don't want to get into the alphabet at all. Find a new response. One that empowers how you want to live, one that indicates to you that you can handle your emotions; they are not in charge of you.

STORY

A woman, married for five years and very much in love with her husband, discovered that he had been having a sexual relationship with another woman. She was hurt, angry, and confused. In the midst of all the emotion she made a decision never to trust him again. She confronted him with the knowledge, and he admitted that it was true. He told her that he still loved her and wanted to remain with her; he also said that he would not do this again.

Six years later, true to his word, he had not been unfaithful again. However, his wife had begun to arrange her life around her decision to never trust him again. There was not a place in their relationship that was not colored by this decision. She put a little distance between them so that he would not hurt her so badly again. She found herself unable to love him unconditionally as she had before. The relationship had less and less energy, and they found themselves, six years later, becoming strangers.

COMMENT

From the place of not trusting, it is impossible to fully invest oneself in a relationship. Sometimes the situation is so insidious that you even forget that you made such an emotional decision, and you are left with a very small space to relate in. The best remedy, of course, is prevention: Never make an important decision in the midst of emotion. As time passes and the emotion fades, you are left with a decision that may be quite unrelated to the current situation.

THE BIG IDEA

Emotions make you heavy and burdened, while feelings, even difficult ones like sadness, lighten you up.

What emotions paralyze you? Why?

What emotional encounters are familiar to you?

What feelings do you recognize that are
obviously generated from the inside?

How do you recognize your feelings?

How have you handled a devastating
emotion in the past?

Do you have an old emotion that is easily
triggered?

What can you do differently about it?

What does the little you on your shoulder tell
you about your feelings?

Mind Your Mind

Intention: To use your mind as a tool

TALKING ABOUT LIFE

Watch your mind. It is like a monkey—it jumps from thought branch to thought branch. Many times you might find that your mind is running the show, jumping from idea to idea, from thought to thought, often without your control.

Think of the times you didn't want to think about something. Remember how that very thing kept popping into your mind, consuming the space of your thoughts, dictating that you would, in fact, think about the very thing that you didn't want to think about.

Your mind is a tool for expressing your essence in the world. It is a great tool for balancing your checkbook or deciding what brand of television to buy, but it is inadequate in telling you how to live. Whenever you find yourself stuck, or thinking in ways that are limiting, your mind has probably been deciding how you should live your life.

Unattended, your mind will latch onto any old piece of content and think about it. It will take you down roads you no longer wish to travel. Your mind can start down a road of the past that leads you to depression. Your mind can start down roads that lead to anger. Your mind prob-

You can

think what

you

want.

ably has some pet projects of its own—things it likes to think about. Many times, however, when you examine the thoughts your mind likes to hang out with, you will realize that those aren't the thoughts that give you a great life. They are often thoughts that end up in "I can't" or "I'm not good enough," or many other self-defeating deadends. Your mind thinks that you have to think what *it* wants you to think, and often in life we just follow the thought trails of our minds.

However, you don't have to think about what your mind chooses. You can choose to think what you want. If you know that thinking X leads you to call out your smallest self, decide that you will think Y instead. You will know if you are thinking the thoughts that you want because you will lighten up.

You pick the topics you want to think about. Put your mind on what you want to think about. Talk to your mind. You might say, if your mind is terribly persistent, "I'll think about this to-morrow." Or say to your mind, "Thank you for sharing. I'm now going to think what I want."

The problem with letting your mind run your life is that it often does not have your greatest interest at heart. Your mind may be in the habit of thinking self-defeating thoughts, and if you follow your mind down those paths, it convinces you that you can't.

Start to notice the workings of your mind. Find its favorite haunts. Look at these and see if these thoughts are ones that call forth your Purposed Self. Think what you want to think.

STORY

A woman confided in her friend that she was worried her husband was developing a friendship with another woman. She did not think that he was actually having an affair, but a friendship was definitely forming and the husband shared this development with her. Although the woman knew that this was not a comfortable situation for her, she wanted to be understanding and supportive of her husband's life.

First and foremost she considered her relationship with her husband a friendship and she realized that as a friend she wanted him to be happy and full. She did not think about her other friends, "This is my friend and I don't think that she should have a friendship with X." It seemed ridiculous to have such judgments about their lives. Yet, when she thought about her husband's friend, she became distinctly uncomfortable. She told herself that if she planned to live another forty years or so with this man, she could not expect that he would never make a new friendship. She would not wish this on any of her other friends.

The woman realized that her discomfort was not only making her miserable, but it was also affecting the quality of her relationship. She noticed that if she let her mind think about this situation randomly, she could work herself into a frenzy of worry. However, if she chose what she wanted her mind to be thinking, she would always opt for remembering that her husband was her friend and what she wanted most for him was that he love his life.

You are not your mind. You don't have to think about what your mind chooses. Think about what *you* want to think about. Think those things that lighten up your life.

THE BIG IDEA

Mind your mind.

What does your mind think that you don't want to think?

How often does your mind think about things you don't want to think about?

What can *you* do to help you think what you want (such as turn off the soap opera)?

What regular themes does your mind insist on thinking?

How can you remember to notice what your mind is thinking?

Change

Intention: To give you peace of mind

TALKING ABOUT LIFE

Change is an internal process that manifests in our external reality. It is the movement of experience that propels you forward, growing on every level. Your body is changing, constantly shedding dead cells and rebuilding new ones. Your emotions change with the stimulus of your life's content. You often change your mind about any given subject.

Since change is so ongoing and natural, how is it that people resist, deny, and avoid change with such great fervor? How is it that a natural process conjures up such fear and loathing? The truth is that change is not what hurts you. It is the consistent denial of change that causes problems and pain. Your struggle to maintain the status quo, to keep peace, to avoid rocking the boat is what blocks the internal process of natural growth.

Your mind continues to hang on to the familiar because your mind does not like change. Your mind thinks that danger lurks in the unknown, and it wants no part of it. Your mind has the illusion that change is dangerous. It has rushed to get you settled; it wants things handled in your life, as if handled would bring happiness. Just at the moment when you think you've got your life handled, you may notice discontent brewing inside of you. This discontent is your growth wanting to happen. It is your Purposed Self asking for a change, a new experience to move you along in life. Do you really want to get to the end of change? That is, to the end of growth, of new experiences, of challenge? When you love your life, change is welcomed because you know it calls forth a greater opportunity to add to the life you love.

Sometimes change is nothing more than getting at peace with the life you have. It is a quiet force asking you to live your greatest and to follow the steps necessary to promote your well being. It might be a question, or a knowing that now is the time for a change.

STORY

A woman was depressed and unhappy with her life. Day after day went by, and she did the same things, which she believed didn't amount to much. She wasn't interested in her job, and her friends bored her. She had thought many times about doing something about her life but she just couldn't cope with the idea of change. Change had always frightened her because of the unknown.

Finally, she could stand it no more. She decided that it would give her a lift in life to get a new job. After three months on the new job, she still found herself unhappy. Next, she decided to meet some new people. She busied herself with single's clubs, but she still wasn't satisfied. So she decided to sell her house and move. The process took her several months and provided a lot of distractions. While she liked her new home, she still had the issue of depression. She couldn't imagine what was wrong. After all, she had rearranged all of her content.

COMMENT

All natural change is connected to a greater force that complements the whole of life. What can you do, who can you be, if you welcome change as a guide? To live the whole of your life requires persistent, never ending, change.

THE BIG IDEA

Change is a natural process of living. Its consequence is growth.

What three changes have you made in the past that have facilitated your growth?

What was your experience before the change and after the change? In what way did you come to know, trust, and love yourself?

What can you do when you realize that you need change?

What change is going on in your life right now?

Living On Purpose

Life Purpose

Thinking Big About Your Life

Intention: To inspire you

TALKING ABOUT LIFE

Children know how to imagine. They have
their whole life in front of them. They are consistently told, "You can be anything you want to
be when you grow up." They dream big dreams.
They pretend they have it all. The only thing that
stands in the way of manifesting their dreams is
time—time to make that which they have dreamed about reality.

You can dream big dreams and think big
thoughts. It takes very little imagination on your
part. The only thing that stands in your way is
you. Remember what you wanted when you had
your whole life in front of you. Did you manifest
what you wanted? What happened?

It is fascinating how people forget to think big
about themselves and their lives. You can blame
it on circumstances, you can blame others, but
the real problem is you.   The good news is that
you can stop looking for the culprit who stole
your dreams and think again.

It is never too late to think big. As a matter of
fact, you have nothing to lose and everything to
gain with this mode of thinking. And you must
think big in order to discover your Life Purpose.
Stretch your mind's thinking about yourself.
You must look beyond the content of your life and

Are you

thinking

big

enough?

the limitations you believe about it.

You can begin by imagining that you have a clean slate. You have the rest of your life in front of you. You hold no grudges and no grudges are held against you. You want to live a life that matters, and fortunately you do have a life that matters. You can have or do whatever you like. Imagine yourself as someone who is going to make a contribution to life. How big can you think? What would you want to do?

The truth is, you do have a big life. It's just that you forgot to notice. You make a contribution, but you don't count it. What if you looked at your life as fresh and as clear as you did when you first fell in love? Remember how enamored you were with this person? Now focus that same fascination on yourself. Find out who you are. Look at yourself much bigger than you have been looking.

If you already see yourself as someone born for a reason, look bigger. Think bigger about yourself. You are not exempt from seeing yourself too small. If you are not fulfilled by your life, you must stretch your thinking about yourself. Your Life Purpose lives where you see yourself big.

Once you are thinking big about yourself, you can see that it is relatively painless. You have nothing to lose. You will get fresh ideas about yourself and your life. You will begin anew today, by thinking big about yourself and what you want to do with your moments. The moments add up to your life. What thoughts are you thinking while the moments are passing away?

STORY

A young boy had a vivid imagination. He believed he would grow up and be a great politician. He had a difficult childhood, but he was able to maintain his dream throughout high school. This was a challenging time because he didn't have support for going to college. And he had fallen in love.

This young man had big decisions to make that would affect the rest of his life. He opted for love and a good job. As the years passed he forgot his dream. He had a family to support and the bills kept coming in. The older he got, the less fulfilled he became.

However, something in his head kept nagging at him. What about being a politician? He was a good leader, but his participation in organizations hadn't fulfilled his political ambitions. He loved people and they constantly wanted him to join in. When others looked at his life, it seemed as if he had the perfect life. But he knew his capabilities.

One day he remembered his dream. What had happened? He understood that he had stopped dreaming or thinking big at all.

COMMENT

You cannot be bigger than you can think. If you want more in your life, you must stretch yourself and think bigger. Your life is made up of those things you have thought about it. Your Life Purpose lives where you think big.

THE BIG IDEA

Your dreams can become reality, so make sure you are thinking big enough.

What are you passionate about?

What moments were you fully enrolled in your life today?

What are the most unusual things about you?

What are three possibilities open to you when you think big?

Getting A Life

Intention: To stop waiting and start living

TALKING ABOUT LIFE

Are you waiting for something to happen or someone to change before you consider your life? Or are you at the end of a responsibility or relationship and don't know what to do? The issue with waiting is hoping and the issue with the end is beginning.

Life never runs out of opportunities for you to experience and grow. If you have recently been retired, widowed, or divorced, or your children are now grown, you may feel at odds with the new situation. If you insist on waiting and staying stuck in endings, how much of your life will you be missing? When you find yourself confronting a dead end, it is an opportunity to get yourself a life.

Sometimes it happens that you wait your whole life to get to the end of something, when you will then do X, Y, or Z. Then the time comes and you notice that the courage you once had has disappeared. Or maybe you have always shared your life with someone who is no longer there and you find yourself at a loss.

If you are waiting for something to happen, you may notice that the something that is happening is nothing. You can sit back while more years pass or you can begin to make decisions. It is up to you to get yourself a life. Rarely do bands come marching down the street to tell you what to do.

If you are living on past memories, or future hopes and wishes, your life is passing away. Begin where you are in order to get yourself a life. Decide what quality of life you want and make decisions that will point you in that direction. Does it matter if you have to start over? All there is about starting over is taking the opportunity to live more of your life. No matter what your circumstance is, you don't want to miss a second of the life you have to live.

It has always been up to you to get a life. There just isn't anyone else that can get a life for you. If you are unhappy or dissatisfied, decide what life you want to live now. Look at it as another choice, another chance to create a life that you love. The real joy is in the getting of your life. You choose X because it is in your life's best interest. You decide Y because that's what would please you. You want to stop waiting and wishing and get yourself a life now, because life is not over until you die.

STORY

A man had finally reached his day of retirement. He had worked hard most of his life and now he would be able to relax. The first few weeks he got up when he wanted, played golf on weekdays, and spent time with his wife. He was fascinated with this unusual routine and it did seem to keep him busy.

A year passed and the novelty wore off. His day had always started at 6:00 a.m. and now it started at 10:00 a.m. Although he liked golf, he wasn't satisfied. He loved his wife but he wasn't fulfilled living the content of her life. Slowly he began to drop out of life. He stayed home more often and his discontent grew. He felt it was too late for him to begin a new career and he didn't need the income.

Another year passed and he missed working. His unstructured days left him feeling useless and old. He became irritable with his wife and friends and they began to avoid him. His isolation was growing and his depression was becoming critical.

One day a neighbor asked if he could use the man's workshop. The man hadn't been in it in over a year. The neighbor was making a hobby horse for his young son and hoped to have it finished by Christmas. The man realized the neighbor wouldn't have it finished in time. He offered to help out because he had lots of time and he was good at woodworking.

He completed the toy on time and the neighbor was thrilled. It was so good that other friends and neighbors wanted wood toys for their children and grandchildren. His participation with the neighbor could be the very thing that gives him the opportunity to get a life now.

COMMENT

Getting a life is about living. It is never too soon or too late to start considering what would make a great life for you. Years can pass while you are waiting for something to happen or wishing things weren't as they are. So make the decision you need to make and begin something that would give you a life.

THE BIG IDEA

Your life is not over until it's over.

What decisions do you need to make to get yourself a life?

What have you been wishing hadn't happened?

What have you been hoping would happen?

How does the above relate to your getting a life?

When did you think you would be finished getting a life?

Is there some resentment you have about starting anew?

Does that resentment keep you from getting a life?

When was a time you stopped waiting?

What Is Life Purpose?

Intention: To discover your Life Purpose

TALKING ABOUT LIFE

It is not a job.

As you begin to work through this section, it is important to understand what you are looking for. First, you need to come to terms with the fact that you are not searching for a job or career. If your mind is made up that what you need is a new job or a solid career to fulfill yourself, you will be limiting your ability to see yourself as someone born with a Purpose.

You will want to ease your mind's concerns by imagining for awhile. Imagine, for instance, that you already have all you need to live a fulfilling life. Tell your mind that a job or career is not the issue right now. You are looking for a new idea about yourself. You want to discover something that makes your whole life fit, that explains how you have lived and how you will continue to live. You will be looking for an expression about yourself that says it all about you.

You were not born for nothing.

It may or may not be a new idea that you were born for a reason, for some Purpose. If you have never considered the idea that you have a Life Purpose, now is the time to tell your mind you are going to think in a new way for awhile. You may notice that your mind cannot comprehend what you could be searching for. Your mind may start some intense arguing about who it thinks you are, but you are not concerned because you are now curious about this new idea that you were born for a Purpose.

You may be someone who has always felt inside that there is some meaning to your life, and you would be thrilled to live with a Purpose if only you could identify it. You know you have been searching for some Purpose that would really fulfill you in a way that no other content has. You may notice that some elusive feeling has been calling you to contribute something and you really want to. Tell your mind that you are going to look at yourself more objectively than you ever have. It may mean that you see yourself as more impactful than you have ever admitted or dared notice.

Whatever your present position is about yourself, relax. There is a place deep inside of you that would love to believe that you were born for something. You do not even have to create a place of belief, because it is just a fact that you have a Life Purpose. If you look at your life for a moment and if you count what you do, you will know that you were not born for nothing.

You can discover it when you look at yourself On Purpose.

Living On Purpose means you do not judge

Living On Purpose

yourself, thereby discounting what is about you. If you have a habit of telling yourself nothing you do counts or you did it wrong or your dearest friend's acknowledgments don't count or you don't deserve recognition, you must stop it right now.

Admit to yourself that fundamentally you are tired of being so difficult on yourself. Admit that you would truly like to think of yourself as a magnificent human being. Admit that, when all is said and done, you would just like to feel great about other people and about yourself. Admit that it takes a lot of energy to keep beating yourself down, and that you don't even like other people too much when you continue to judge yourself so harshly.

This is the time to ease up on yourself, to be gentle in your thoughts about yourself. Start thinking in terms of "I really am a wonderful person who has something to contribute to this life." Tell yourself you are now going to have some compassion and understanding for yourself. You are going to discover something about yourself that is inspiring because you are going to look at yourself On Purpose, which is without judgment.

Look big.

The reason most people have difficulty in discovering their Life Purpose is because they do not see themselves big enough. Some people recognize their Life Purpose and then they say, "This is too big for me. It makes me uncomfortable."

What have you got to lose thinking big about yourself? You could consider it a dream or fantasy. Fantasize for a moment about who you would like to be and what you would like to contribute. Think big about your power and what you would intend to do with it.

The single biggest obstacle in thinking big about yourself is your judgments about your content. Your mind tells you that you don't amount to much because you are constantly upset with so and so, you get depressed, no one loves you, you are afraid, you are not understood, you never get your share, and, besides, your life couldn't possibly be in this condition if you were really up to something big in the world.

Thinking big about yourself means coming to terms with the fact that, whether you like it or not, it makes a difference that *you* are living this life. You may never have shared a golden moment with anyone and still it makes a difference that you are here, living this moment, on this planet. Thinking big simply means that from this moment on you realize that you contribute something very special. Your special something wants you to count it. It's that larger part of yourself that is asking you to stop thinking that you don't amount to much, and start living and sharing as if you had a big life.

It's about discovering something you already have.

The wonderful thing about your Life Purpose is that you already have it. You are not going to discover some unfamiliar thing about yourself that you could never do. You already do it, and you already know many things about it.

Discovering your Life Purpose is actually a process of self-discovery and self-acceptance. You come to value what you already possess and have always possessed. It may be that you have so discounted what is important to you that you have lost sight of your most valuable attribute. It may be that your mind thinks that only special people have a Life Purpose, and you have never considered yourself special.

Whatever you have been thinking, now you are thinking about yourself in a new way. You are realizing that there is something about you that is quite unique and special. You have a Life Purpose that is familiar to you, and now you understand that it means something to other people when you share it. It doesn't even require that you get something else, such as more knowledge, more experience, or more patience. It simply requires that you begin to value what there already is about you. You understand that your life is as significant as anyone else's and you intend to acknowledge that fact.

It's a quality that you want to center your life around.

When you claim your significance, you begin to notice that there are times when you feel especially good about yourself. Further, there is a subtle drive to create more of those times. You feel as if people need you and appreciate your special efforts. You may begin to notice that you have wanted the right job, the right relationship, the right life. Notice, now, why exactly do you want the right content? Does your mind believe if only you had the right content you could be more of how you want to be?

When you are aware of yourself, you are able to notice many important things about your life. You are at choice about how you want to be. It is not a surprise to you that you want to express the best of yourself. In many ways you have centered your life around you wanting to feel good about yourself and others. Remember those times you felt best about yourself, and see if you haven't tried to create a life that makes you feel good all the time.

Maybe you didn't notice that you did something that made you feel wonderful. Maybe you thought it was the circumstance. Feeling good happens from the inside out. Notice what came from the inside of you that created the experience on the outside. You have spent your life wanting to recreate those experiences that make you feel great. Now you must accept the fact that *you* made you feel great and you must discover what *you* did to make that happen.

You may have noticed your Life Purpose during peak experiences.

Sometimes you have had experiences that you recognize as peak experiences. A peak experience is a moment that you touch something inside of you that you recognize as excellent. It is a moment of realizing the wonder of being alive. You are filled with yourself. You understand your life as one of significance. You know your being is important, and you feel peaceful and fulfilled. Those moments make a difference to you because you experience that you make a difference. The question is, what happened that created such a profound experience? Where did this feeling come from and will you ever experience it again?

When you know your Life Purpose you have a vehicle that enables you to tap into the best of yourself, and then you are at choice about expressing it or not. Expressing your greatness leaves you with the feeling that you have contributed. The content of your contribution need not be judged because all sharing of your greatness counts as a contribution. Each contribution makes a difference. To create a peak experience, you touch your greatness and share it.

Life Purpose is natural and spontaneous.

Life Purpose is a quality that you express naturally and spontaneously. Remember those times when people you care about wanted you to share with them? Maybe they were in need and asked you for your contribution. Think about what you do especially well and what you want to contribute naturally. What do you want others to get that would make a difference for them? What is it that you see naturally, that you would like them to see for themselves?

You give it of yourself.

By now you may be realizing that you do have something to offer just because you are alive. You may have a hint that you have been given an extraordinary gift to give to others. In fact, others seek you out because they know you have knowledge that will benefit them.

When you interact with others specifically to give of yourself, you will give them your Life Purpose. This means that you have a natural ability to express your knowledge in such a way that the other person has an experience inside. You can recognize those times that someone understood inside what you wanted them to know about themselves. And you know if they got what you wanted to give to them or not. Sometimes you are persistent and they have a great encounter with your Life Purpose.

Your Life Purpose is a gift because you get something for yourself when you interact On

Purpose. And it is a gift to others because they get something from you that is theirs to keep. They have an experience inside that shifts their reality.

These are examples of Life Purposes that some people have discovered.

to enable	to inspire	to challenge
to awaken	to help	to produce
to direct	to understand	to counsel
to achieve	to master	to empower
to ignite	to journey	to seek
to participate	to relate	to listen
to synthesize	to intuit	to befriend
to organize	to negotiate	to validate
to create	to share	to energize
to teach	to heal	to liberate
to support	to love	to enhance
to enlighten	to accept	to design

COMMENT

If you want to discover your Life Purpose, you must think of yourself in a new way.

THE BIG IDEA

Everyone was born with a Life Purpose.

Everyone has a Life Purpose that can be specifically identified and named. Life Purpose is the quality about you that is unique and powerful. You express it naturally and spontaneously. Right now, without further work or education, you are an expert in the area of your Life Purpose. Life Purpose is a gift, a gift given to you to give away to others. Knowing your Life Purpose gives definition to who you are and enables you to glimpse your larger mission. When acknowledged, Life Purpose creates significance in your life.

As you begin to search for your Life Purpose, you need to be On Purpose. Remember that you are not going to discount your true greatness by judging yourself. You will think of yourself in the most generous of ways. You will be re-creating your grandest moments.

You will be looking for an active quality. There is something you do that comes from the inside of you that you actively want to create for others. It may be something you want them to know about themselves or something you want them to have for themselves. When you tell the truth, you want people to have great lives all the time. And if you thought you could, you would want to give them what you believe it would take for them to have great lives.

Do not think too much about the answers to these questions. Thinking leads you to a lot of judgments about yourself. Pick a quiet time of introspection and let the answers just come to you. Your Purposed Self knows the answers. Do not concern yourself about repetitive answers.

Living On Purpose   195

1. What quality about you is most unique?
You are not necessarily looking for a talent. You are looking deep inside to discover what you believe is special or what others tell you is special about you. You *know* that no one else experiences this quality exactly like you do. Try to visualize your uniqueness by seeing yourself as others would experience you, not by how you would judge yourself.

2. Why do people want you in their life?
Sometimes they tell you what your presence in their life means to them, and sometimes you can only tell by their actions. Look for the special things about you that cause other people to want you in their life.

3. What quality do you give others that they consider to be your strongest asset?
Sometimes you hear from a third party that someone thinks you are very special in a particular way. Sometimes others will tell you that you are special because you give X. Look for that quality about you that is recognizable to others.

4. What quality do you give when you are relating at your best?

Sometimes your magnificence springs forth unexpectedly. Other times you purposefully want others to see you at your best. Either way, look for the times that you knew the best of you was present for the situation. You felt full and good about yourself because you knew something special happened.

5. What do people always say about you?

You always make others laugh, lighten up, feel safe, or so on. When other people want to acknowledge you, what do they say?

6. What quality is it that shows up spontaneously and naturally?

You always see X in the situation. You naturally know what people need to enhance their life, solve their problem, ease their concern.

7. What quality makes you feel really alive and wonderful when you express yourself?
Perhaps you invite someone over, something happens, and a live wonderful energy is generated. Or, maybe you went that extra mile for someone and you felt full and great about yourself.

8. What do you most value in yourself?
This is a quality that you recognize expresses your greatest self. You know it because of the way it makes you feel about yourself. You know your fundamental worth by your ability to identify yourself as someone who does X. You know you can contribute by giving X.

9. What is the quality that, for as long as you can remember, has been true about you?
This quality shows up as something you are constantly wanting to offer to others. You may recognize your Life Purpose as a concern you have for others, one that you wish and hope can influence them in some way. When you consider it, you realize that you have always tried to make a difference by something you give.

10. What quality is most evident when you are being the most powerful?

Sometimes you have an encounter with another and you suddenly realize that you told them something, did something, or gave them an idea or experience that truly made a difference in the quality of their life at the moment. You may think, "Did I really do that, say that, or contribute that? Was I really that influential?" Your influence is your power and when you really turn your attention to an interaction with someone, you make a difference to them. What do you do?

11. Why do people want you as a friend?

Why do others tell you in their expressions or in words that you are important to them? You are looking for that quality about yourself that makes your friendship a real treasure.

12. What quality do you possess that could be of real service to others if you paid attention to what you are doing?

When you are being of service, what quality is being expressed?

As you consider your responses, you will begin to see a doorway to knowing yourself as someone who has a gift. Consider for a moment who you are thinking about. Is this person a stranger to you? Or, are you beginning to know this person intimately? What great thing can you come to know about yourself? The following directions will help you find a word that describes your Life Purpose.

Let yourself begin to relax.

Let your thoughts flow in and out without following them.

Take three very deep breaths, exhaling slowly.

Relax your mind and body deeper.

Fill yourself with high esteem that originates from inside.

Visualize yourself looking in a great dictionary of Purposes. Scan this book carefully until you find a word that describes your unique Life Purpose.

Remember not to judge.

What is your Life Purpose?

How Do You Do?

Intention: To see how you are

TALKING ABOUT LIFE

As you look more closely at yourself, you will notice the difference between your Life Purpose and your Life Energy. Your Life Purpose is interactive and your Life Energy is definitive. It is important to know the difference so that you can accept how you do naturally and what you do naturally.

When you participate with others you have the potential to offer your expertise, your Life Purpose. You have available to you a unique knowledge that can benefit others when you want to make a difference to them. You recognize that it is your Life Purpose that has been expressed because you feel as if you gave and received something during your encounter with them.

In contrast your Life Energy can be recognized whether you are interacting or not. Among other things, your Energy is visibly characterized by how you posture yourself in the world, by particulars that you consider important, by the ways you process information, and by your persona.

There

is

nothing

wrong.

Posture

If you have Aliveness Energy, you have a vivacious posture, while the Energy of Workability presents a confident posture. Truth Energy is expressed through an independent posture.

Particulars

Familiarity is one of the most important particulars that Aliveness Energy values. Workability Energy favors efficiency and Truth Energy is partial to significance.

Process

When people with Aliveness Energy process information, they feel and respond. People with Workability energy, on the other hand, process by tracking and anticipating, while people with Truth Energy more naturally notice and reconcile.

Persona

Spirited typifies the Aliveness Energy persona, and conscientious describes Workability Energy's. The persona of Truth Energy, however, is better described as intuitive.

There are other ways to differentiate between Life Purpose and Life Energy. Life Purpose asks you to do something with your life, while Life Energy tells you something about yourself. For instance, Life Purpose might ask you to empower others to accept change. Life Energy might tell you that you are understanding and accepting. A person with Truth Energy whose Life Purpose is "to change," for example, might have a powerful ability to understand. This may explain why they occasionally find themself supporting opposing camps. They have an ability to accept each side where it is, and yet they seem to know what changes are needed from both sides to move beyond the issues.

When you know your Life Energy, you can liberate yourself by loving the way you are. Loving your Life Energy begins an integration process that enables you to become a vehicle for the expression of your Life Purpose. For example, sometimes your Life Purpose knows what is needed to help in situations that you have few ideas about. It is important to love your Energy because you will have fewer judgments about yourself that inhibit the expression of your Life Purpose.

STORY

A woman whose Life Purpose was companionship was unhappy with her life. She was very fond of people and through the years she had been married and divorced several times. With each new relationship she felt committed for life. However, someone new would enter her life and she would soon end up being more than a friend.

She had Aliveness Energy and was feeling critical of herself. She couldn't understand why her relationships didn't work. But even when they were legally ended, she found herself continuing to be involved in them. She was in a constant struggle to keep her distance because they all sought her companionship.

She didn't understand that her Life Energy kept her interested in people, people, and more people. Added to this was the fact that people close to her adored her because she could give companionship that had a positive influence on their lives.

COMMENT

Life Purpose and Life Energy are distinctly different. Life Purpose explains what you are meant to do and Life Energy explains how you do.

THE BIG IDEA

Love your Life Energy and then your Life Purpose will find the interactions where it can make the difference.

What are the distinctions between your Life Purpose and your Life Energy?

When you experience loving how you do, how do you want to interact with people?

What is most important to you about how you do?

What is most important to you about what you give to others?

Don't Tone It Down

Intention: To live boldly

TALKING ABOUT LIFE

Toning It Down is what has happened when you recognize that your experience of your current self is less than your experience of your greatest self. Your experience of your greatest self is more than your experience of your current self. To find out if you are Toning It Down, look at your experience.

Toning It Down is toning down your essence. Toning It Down is toning down the very thing that makes you who you are. It is toning down your essential being. Tone It Down has been heard as "Don't make waves" and "Don't rock the boat." Don't impact at all.

You know that you can walk through the aisles of the grocery store so toned down that nobody will have seen you. Probably you are also aware that some people walk through the aisles of family, marriage, church, school, and neighborhood so toned down that they don't leave an imprint, for days or even years on end. No waves. No rocking.

A Purposed life is lived boldly. It is not toned down. When you are On Purpose, you want your experience of current living to be as great as you know your experience of greatest living to be.

One problem about Toning It Down is that it

becomes a habit. First you tone down one thing for one situation or for one audience, and then you tone down another, and another, and so it spreads. The more areas you tone down, the fewer the areas where you experience your greatest self. You love your life when you are experiencing life from your greatest self. The further away from your greatest self you experience life, the less you love it.

Another problem about Toning It Down is that there are no seams. As you tone down, even if only in one area, it affects all other areas of your life. Another problem is that it makes you extremely unbalanced in the world. You have to behave one way in one place and another way in another place. If you have to jump into your toned down self whenever you see X, it can be disorienting. If, after you have toned it down, you attempt to leap back into your greatest self, it can be very difficult.

Another problem is that we often tone down in the very experiences that our greatest self wants most to have—in our primary relationships; in our families; in our work; with our gods. Toning It Down where it matters the most deprives you of having a life you love. Toning It Down is exhausting, doesn't get you anywhere, and is, finally, boring. The more toned down you are, the less energy you have.

When your current experience of life is your greatest experience of self, you know you have not toned it down. You are playing full out— 100%. You know how magnificently you are capable of experiencing your life.

The thing is, when you don't Tone It Down, you astound yourself. You really are who your greatest self knows you are. When you don't Tone It Down, your current experience of your life is an experience recognized and loved by your greatest self. When you don't Tone It Down, you find out that you know things you didn't know you knew. You find out you can do things you didn't know you could do. You find out that your experience of your life is as great as you dreamed it could be. You are filled.

STORY

A man was astounding at work. He was successful, respected, and liked. He amazed himself at how wonderful he had become. He loved the experience of being himself at work, for there his greatest self came out to play. However, when he left work, he left his greatest self in his desk drawer. He engaged less with his children than his clients, less with his wife than his boss. He toned it down at home. He toned it so far down at home that he was almost dead. His experience of himself at home was less than his experience of himself at work. He never showed up at home.

COMMENT

It's your life. How many parts of it have you toned down?

THE BIG IDEA

When you don't Tone It Down, you will really pull it off.

How far down have you toned your life?

Do you have a habit of Toning It Down with certain people or in certain situations?

What would it take to not Tone It Down habitually?

With whom and in what circumstances does your greatest self show up?

One day this week, deliberately don't Tone It Down. Notice the experience.

A Major Expression

TALKING ABOUT LIFE

After you have defined your Life Purpose you will want to become aware of its expression. You will notice all the details about it. You will see it spring forth naturally and spontaneously. When you give it credibility, you will see that it is your contribution and place of power.

You will notice that knowing your Life Purpose makes a difference in your interactions with people. It makes a difference in how you want others to experience you and in how you want to experience your life. All of these awarenesses cause a desire to grow inside of you—a desire to embrace that which makes you feel like you have a reason for being.

You may notice that you want to spend the greatest portion of your time expressing that which makes you feel fulfilled. You want to give the best of yourself and you want others to know the best of you. You may realize that you want a major expression for your Life Purpose. You may find yourself wanting to give of yourself, beyond your present boundaries.

Your personal growth enhances the power of your Life Purpose. Every time you recognize when you give the expertise of your Life Purpose you become more powerful, as does your Life

Real

expression

has

passion.

Purpose. This is a natural process of evolution. You are evolving, and your Life Purpose is becoming more and more profound.

A major expression begins to unfold when you count that your gift can be of influence in lives. You will want to know your Life Purpose intimately. You will need to admit that you want to be up to something. It will begin to guide you because you value the power of it in the same way that you value yourself. There is no separation between how you think of yourself and how you think of your Life Purpose.

Because Life Purpose is your gift to give of yourself, you will naturally want to make a contribution by expressing it. Say yes to the opportunities that make you feel that you are contributing. Do what makes you feel light. Stretch yourself. Get out in the open. You can count on yourself when you trust your Life Purpose. Count the expression you have for your Life Purpose as the major one right now. Know that your Life Purpose will lead you to greater and greater expressions when you make each encounter with it the most important one. You will come to a major expression that is more fulfilling than you dared dream possible. Your greatness will have its expression.

STORY

A woman identified her Life Purpose as "to create." She had an ability to transform the most unusual remnants into a work of art. She chose natural material from the environment to create everything from simple handiwork to decorative ornaments. She was rarely without requests from family, friends, and strangers for her creations.

Unfortunately, she found herself divorced with two children to support. She had some office experience and an acquaintance hired her to work for a small business that was growing. Months went by and she was working hard to get ahead. All her attention was concentrated on her job and her art work was put away. The business thrived and eventually she was promoted to office manager, but she was not happy.

During her vacation she was going through her closets and she saw many projects in mid-creation. Her enthusiasm surprised her and she spent the rest of her vacation finishing several pieces she loved. When her vacation was over she was at a turning point. She realized that she had been satisfied and fulfilled for the first time in months. She knew she loved to create everything from clothes to art pieces for others to enjoy. Even though it seemed risky, she began looking for ways to express her Life Purpose that would support her spending the majority of her time creating.

COMMENT

The more your value your Life Purpose, the more you will want to stretch yourself to express it. Start by valuing each encounter with your Life Purpose as a major expression. When you become an expert at expressing your Life Purpose in one situation, begin to look for ways to stretch yourself into other situations. Let it challenge you to get further out.

THE BIG IDEA

If you take your Life Purpose seriously, it demands a major expression.

In what areas do you minorly express your Life Purpose?

In what areas do you know you could majorly express your Life Purpose but you just haven't yet?

In what other areas would you love to give the gift of your Life Purpose?

Where can you stretch yourself?

Tugging On Your Sleeve

Intention: To notice when to give

TALKING ABOUT LIFE

Eventually you understand about the power you are sharing when you express your Life Purpose. Many times your Life Purpose is expressed as a small gesture, and other times it is expressed as an irreversible encounter. However your Life Purpose is expressed, you want it to be a gift to whomever it is directed.

A gift is only a gift when it is received. If you are insistent that someone receive the gift of your Life Purpose when they aren't asking, it is not a gift at all. Your efforts are diminished because others are not receptive to it, and your good intentions are shaken.

Expressing your Life Purpose means sharing it. You want to listen during your encounters for the moments that you can make a difference. These times will present themselves, because others want what you can give. Let them ask you by tugging on your sleeve. They will ask you for small things, and at other times they will ask you to make an intervention. Whatever it is they want, wait, watch, and listen for the tug.

Maybe they have a problem and you have a solution. Maybe they want to obtain something and you know exactly what they should do. Then

They must

rip

your sleeve

off.

again, they might be in crisis and they call you for help. Sometimes they need encouragement, support, caring, nurturing, leading, love, and guidance, and they ask you to empower them through the expression of your Life Purpose.

You want to give the best of yourself by expressing your Life Purpose deliberately. Your intention to empower by expressing your Life Purpose lightens your experience. You become riveted to their communications. Are they tugging on your sleeve? Is it time for you to act?

Your Life Purpose tells you that you were born for something. You want all of the interactions of your Life Purpose to count. You want others to know that you are serious about your sharing. You want them to know you will be happy to give what you can; however, you will not tolerate your Life Purpose being trivialized. Therefore, you are only going to share what you know is best and only when they are ready to receive this gift. You might even tell them that it is their responsibility to get you to understand that they want the expertise of your Life Purpose.

You don't, any longer, want to throw away encounters that express your Life Purpose. You want to be On Purpose; therefore, you need to wait until others tug on your sleeve before acting. If you are unsure, they must tug harder; if you are still unsure, they must rip your sleeve off. Because if they tug hard enough you are going to go for the big solution, the one that creates an irreversible encounter with them, by giving them the gift of your Life Purpose.

STORY

A man saw his neighbor working in the yard on a project that was quite complicated. He went over to see how it was progressing and observed that the neighbor was doing it in such a way that the problem was not being solved. He shared what he knew about this problem but the neighbor was not interested. In addition, the neighbor became irritated with him for interfering.

The man realized that he had offered his advice without it having been requested—without the neighbor having tugged on his sleeve.

COMMENT

The idea is to give what you have to give at your best, and only when someone is asking. If your Life Purpose is "to lead" and you lead without being invited, it is a burden. If you lead from Purpose, it is a gift. If your Life Purpose is "to master," others can experience their own mastery when you let the know-how come through you. No matter what your Life Purpose is, people who want it will be drawn to you. Wait for them to ask for your expertise; watch for their tug.

It's your choice to respond to those who are tugging on your sleeve, to have encounters that really matter, ones that make you stand out like a beacon. You *choose* to respond to the tugs from your Purposed Self.

THE BIG IDEA

Wait for the tugs, and let the gift come through you. That's the best of you.

When did you most recently notice someone tugging on your sleeve?

When did you express your Life Purpose without someone else tugging on your sleeve? What happened?

When were you trying to gift someone and they couldn't receive it?

In what recent situation could you have contributed where you weren't sure if you should?

What are some of your reactions when others tug on your sleeve?

Have you set limits about responding to someone's tugging?

What have you done On Purpose when someone was tugging on your sleeve?

Stop Trashing

Intention: To give yourself a break

TALKING ABOUT LIFE

What is trashing anyhow? This is how it goes. You talk to a friend and complain at length about your significant other. This thought (complaint) gets energy attached to it and gets sent along the universal grapevine. Ultimately, whether they know the content or not, your significant other knows how you have been speaking about them. A variation upon the theme is when you are in a blue funk about your life. Nothing is going as you planned and you aren't liking your life. You get together with a friend and share (dump) what's up in your life lately. These are both examples of trashing.

There is no innocent gossip. The truth is that seemingly innocent gossip actually affects you and the person you are talking about. So what's the harm in complaining? The harm comes in several ways.

—You talk into being a scenario that you dislike, that of not liking your life. Have your ever noticed how a small thought comes to mind and you put it in your attention and it gets bigger and bigger?

—You add energy to an already shaky situation.

You can escalate a simple irritation into a major battle in this way. You have inflated the issue.

—You have created as "truth" something that is quite fluid. One day your significant other is wonderful and the next, dreadful. The problem with telling the truth in this way is that the fluidity is removed, and you can get stuck at *dreadful* (even when it is only partly the experience).

Have you ever noticed how certain people never trash certain things? The White House staff never trashes the president. They wouldn't have jobs long if they did, and, of course, they don't want to lend energy to potential trouble.

The experience of falling in love is an example of a situation where there is no trashing. Although you know the other person is not perfect, you wouldn't think of dwelling on imperfections, much less give them credibility by talking to someone else about them. The old axiom "divide and conquer" begins with trashing.

STORY

Sara fell in love with David. He is smitten with her as well. They find the time they spend together magical. Even when they are not together there is enormous good will between them. As time passes they find themselves spending more and more time together. They still have good will together, but the magic of it begins to become elusive. Soon small irritations begin to show up and even the space of good will gets shaky. Sara and David decide that they must have a talk. Sara begins by saying she has grown uneasy about their relationship and fears that something is wrong. She says she doesn't know of any specifics but the magic has gone out of it. David agrees that he has also been uneasy and suspects that there is a problem developing.

Almost everyone could add to the development of this story. You begin focusing on the problems and irritations and find to your horror that these problems are getting bigger and filling more of your time than you can tolerate.

COMMENT

Understand the danger in speaking negatively about yourself and others. If you want a great life, one of the things you must do is to think and speak about your life in the most generous terms. Hold it as wonderful, and it will have a shot at being wonderful.

THE BIG IDEA

What not to trash: yourself, your significant other, your children, anything you care about. And don't let anyone else trash them either.

What things about yourself would you like to stop trashing?

What would change in your life if you stopped trashing?

What do you trash about others?

How would your relationships change if you stopped trashing?

Would your job change if you didn't trash it?

Have you accelerated a situation by trashing it?

The Case of Counting It

Intention: To organize your files

TALKING ABOUT LIFE

Have you spent time wondering which experiences really matter? Your life is a series of events that you have participated in and attached some degree of evaluation to. Some experiences you evaluate out of habit, some you take for granted, and others are not familiar enough to label. When you listen to yourself thinking about your experiences, you realize that you are determining what counts and what doesn't. How you count your experiences ultimately creates how you experience your life.

Some things you trash and throw in files called "no good," "more evidence against them," or "they don't love me anymore." Maybe you have been building a case against your significant other. The day they forgot your anniversary you decided that they didn't really care about you. Since that day you have counted petty as well as significant actions as evidence for your case against them.

Or maybe you have a case pending against yourself. You got fired from your job and now you look for evidence that counts against your abilities. When you are thinking about your case, you pull previous files that substantiate

What counts

is

what counts.

Living On Purpose

your most recent experience of failure. Your abilities are counting less and less.

The truth is you have trucks full of files filled with cases for or against your experience of yourself, of others, and of your life. It becomes a real issue when most of your evidence counts negatively about your experiences. If you have a habit of trashing your experiences with someone, ultimately you will find that nothing they do will count in their favor. They could surprise you with a dozen roses and you would count it as evidence that you should be suspicious. If you get desperate, you will enroll others to help you collect more evidence for your case. And you know others are often more than willing to point out negative things that you hadn't noticed.

To have satisfying experiences in your life you will have to count as important what you do and what others do. Collect evidence for files of goodwill. Count the times that your neighbor told you that your child was a gentle person, even if you have files that seem to prove differently.

Count the facts that you got your degree, got promoted six times in six years, manage your home, travel abroad, made another new friend, fixed your own flat tire, remembered to take out the garbage, and didn't hold it against your neighbors when they cut down your rose bush. These experiences count as evidence that you are a wonderful person living a wonderful life. Of course, you will also want to count the facts that your partner bought you a sports car, presented you with diamonds, and tells everyone how wonderful you are; but don't forget to also count that your children told you a secret, let their friend run away to your house, and asked your advice, even if they didn't follow it.

If you want to live a great life, you must reorganize your files of thinking. Begin by looking for what counts to you. If you have predetermined that only a few things count on the positive side, you will have rare occasions to feel great about your life. You can decide how to count experiences of yourself and others. Count the little things, and count the big things. No one else can change your mind if you have already decided that not much counts. This is your life and this is the one that counts for you.

STORY

A young man went away to college, leaving behind a girlfriend that he was serious about. She was finishing her last year of high school and working at a part-time job. They were planning on getting married soon after she graduated.

He had been gone for several months and he missed the young woman. When he first left they talked several times a week on the phone, and wrote letters everyday. The reality of their monthly phone bills made them cut back on their calls. And their lives were busy with many responsibilities.

Often when he called she would be working, running errands, or doing other tasks of living life. He began to get more and more frustrated with her. When they would talk, they argued about the evidence of who loved whom.

As the situation accelerated he began building a case against her. When she tried to call him he would often be gone, but he never counted it. She wrote weekly letters that he began counting as only written out of duty. She didn't sit by the phone and wait for him to call, which he counted as more evidence against her. And, if she shared that she went to dinner with her friends, he was suspicious.

She still loves him and wants to get married. However, he is building his case, and everyone he talks to confirms what he has decided to hear about her.

COMMENT

Become aware of how you have been counting the experiences in your life. You decide what you will count and how you will count it.

THE BIG IDEA

How you count your experiences will determine how you count your life.

What difference would it make in your life if you changed what you count?

What would you like to count as positive, knowing that if you did, it would destroy your case?

What new cases do you have pending and what evidence are you counting?

What do you count as significant evidence that your life matters?

What does your significant other do that matters and how do you count it?

Up And Down The Ladder

Intention: To notice your ups and downs

TALKING ABOUT LIFE

When you are living from your Purposed Self you experience a feeling of fullness and great joy about life. You have a feeling of expanded awareness, and you also have an interest in service to others. You understand that you are an individual with Purpose, and you know that there is a purposefulness to everything about you and your life. Your Purposed Self is not your ego or personality, and there are no judgments about the content of life. Your Purposed Self realizes that a great life does not come from a fine mind or from well expressed emotions. It comes from Purpose.

Your smallest self is constricted in thought and breath. Your emotions are shaky at best, and you have many judgments about yourself, your content, and others. You feel heavy and burdened by life and have little contact with the moment. You can't believe or see the importance of the events of your life, and you can't get this to shift. Your smallest self is about your personality, and your ego wants to run the show. Your mind has stories of justification and self-righteousness for almost any situation, and it is happy to start one for almost any reason.

You may notice that certain people, places, or

events consistently bring out the best of you. Where does the best of you go at other times?

You may remember times in your life when you have had great joy and fulfillment, and you might think those times had little to do with you. You might believe that it was an event or an encounter with a person that made you feel so great.

Actually, others have nothing to do with it. It's you. It's you being On Purpose that makes you feel so great. It takes energy to run up and down the ladder. You go here and get up for it. You go another place and find yourself toning it down. You climb up the ladder to your Purposed Self and then you climb down the ladder to your smallest self.

It is possible to choose where you want to live on the ladder. You can live your life On Purpose by choosing to live up the ladder. To do so, you must make the choice to give up your judgments. You must look at the content that is bothering you and realize that this piece of content is not good or bad, right or wrong, better or worse— this piece of content *just is*. Give up your judgment of how you think it should be, and know that it is just the way it is. Nothing else, no one else can create your having a better or a greater life. The only way to a greater life is to live On Purpose, up the ladder.

STORY

A woman going to school loves the challenge and excitement of it. She wouldn't miss her class for any reason. It's her evening to be who she really is. It is her evening to shine. Every week she climbs up the ladder and goes to class On Purpose. After class she believes her partner, family, and friends would never believe who she is in class, so on the way home she starts climbing down the ladder, getting smaller and smaller.

COMMENT

Climbing down the ladder is an insidious process of the mind. First, you think about what others think of you at your smallest. Then, you decide they may be right. Then, you make up new reasons to prove you don't really count, and that you don't really have any special gifts. From there you practically fall the rest of the way down the ladder to your smallest self.

THE BIG IDEA

You can live a life of fulfillment by remembering your Purposed Self. To do this you must choose to live up the ladder. You do this by giving up your judgments.

How much of your day consists of running up and down the ladder?

Where are the places where you are sure to show up On Purpose?

Name the people in your life who call forth your Purposed Self.

What does it feel like to take steps down the ladder?

What are your present judgments about your life that bring you down the ladder?

Emotional Baggage

Intention: To unpack your suitcase of emotions

TALKING ABOUT LIFE

Have you ever noticed how some people have a favorite piece of emotional baggage? And when you look closer, it becomes obvious that they don't really want to get rid of this baggage. They carry it around on the theory that they would prefer to deal with the devil they know rather than the one they don't. And further, a great segment of their social life revolves around this emotional baggage. They wonder if their friends are calling up for the latest update because it adds a little excitement to their day, or if they are really concerned about the issues.

And soon the emotional baggage is no longer contained in one area; it begins to permeate everywhere. A big problem with emotional baggage is that it eventually takes over your psychic space. When this happens it can pop out at times that you would prefer it didn't. Sometimes this causes problems, and you can no longer count on yourself to live up to your commitments because you have become so involved with your emotional baggage.

On the other hand, you may notice that some people do not carry around a lot of emotional baggage. The fact is that if your psychic space is full of things that help you love your life, there is no room for emotional baggage. The less emotional baggage, the more you tend to love your life. Your smallest self lives committed to your emotional baggage. Your largest self lives On Purpose. Wouldn't it be interesting if you began to introduce yourself from the space of your Life Purpose rather than your problems? What an invitation to your highest self to come out and play.

STORY

On Wednesday mornings each week, several neighbor women gathered to share their lives with each other. One woman had her usual story to tell; each week it was the same. Her only child, a son, had still not called. It was many months now since his last call. Each week she complained about the son and the other women sympathized with her and gave her some ideas about what she could do.

The woman complained profusely but she did nothing about the issue from one week to the next. All the woman was willing to do was to complain about it. She decided that her son was selfish, uncaring, and didn't love her. Her judgment of him was at an all-time low and her judgment of herself was just as low.

What the woman didn't know was that her judgments about herself and her son were the very things that kept her stuck in this issue. What if she just gave up her judgments of her son and called him? What if she gave up expecting him to call? She would have to find something else to fill her attention if she resolved this one.

If you have emotional baggage and wish to get rid of it, drop your judgments about it and get On Purpose. This moves the content out of the realm of emotions and into history.

THE BIG IDEA

You are bigger than your emotions.

What old issues can still upset you when you think about them?

To what extent do old emotions influence you?

What old emotions are you bored with?

What old emotions are your favorites?

When are you going to be finished with your old emotions?

Getting Out Of Your Own Way

Intention: To recognize barriers

TALKING ABOUT LIFE

What does the saying, "Get out of your own way" mean? What needs to get out of the way? Think of the many times you thought, "I can't" or "I don't know," and found that you were stuck. Try as you might, when "I can't" dominates your thoughts, that's the end of possibility. It is these self-limiting and self-defeating ideas that must get out of the way.

You are always at choice about these things. Think of a time when a thought came up and your response was, "I can—I must—I will!" From this place everything is possible. You automatically and instantly begin to look for possibilities. From "I can't" there is no room for possibility. When you get to "I can—I must—I will!" you turn your attention to movement.

There is a difference between the times when "I can't" predominates and the times when "I can—I must—I will!" predominates. When "I can't" is up, your self-esteem is at bottom, and there is *big* trouble. When you are thinking, "I can—I must—I will!" you have already begun looking for what's next to do.

STORY

There was a woman who had a very severe fear of spiders. As long as she could remember she was petrified of them. She was a Girl Scout and chose not to go on camping trips with her friends rather than take the chance of being exposed to spiders. The sight of a spider caused such an instant panic that no amount of rationalizing about it could convince her that she was at choice about this issue.

One day when she was out walking her new baby in its buggy, she looked down to see a large brown spider crawling up the blanket toward the child's exposed hand. She reached in the buggy, picked up the spider, and threw it out. She realized that had this been anything less than protecting her baby she would have fled screaming. It shocked her to know that she had instantly changed her mind about spiders: when pressed, she handled spiders.

COMMENT

What you think is what you create. It is possible to live without the old rules of behavior. When your mind thinks from your personality about an issue, you are in trouble. Stretch beyond the thought "I can't" to the space of "I can—I must—I will!" Do what needs to be done. This is the space of choice, for here the mind is a tool as opposed to a judge. From here Life Purpose becomes reality. You can choose which thoughts support your Purposed Self, and ignore, put down, let go of, set aside, the thoughts that call forth your smallest self.

THE BIG IDEA

If you habitually think, "I can't," you won't. The idea of "I can—I must—I will!" opens a world of possibility and demands action.

How often do you hear yourself say, "I can't"?

How are you limited by "I can't"?

What difference would it make in your life if you stopped saying "I can't"?

What issue will change immediately if you stopped saying "I can't"?

What concerns about yourself are behind "I can't"?

Games Of Purpose

Intention: To lighten the moments

TALKING ABOUT LIFE

You spend much of your life aimlessly busy, going along from place to place. There are hidden moments that you could take advantage of by extending yourself into your world. When you want to give yourself a lift, you can make up wonderful games to play. These are games that give you a clue about living On Purpose.

For example, look around and find out what or who needs your touch. Maybe you could call three friends with some good news. Maybe you could spend one day at home without complaints. Maybe you could drive all the way to work letting other cars in front of you. Another possibility is to tell your significant other a new reason they are important to you. Or you could buy lunch for a friend for no reason; create an elaborate celebration because you lived this day; shoot off firecrackers because you like yourself; get up early to see the sun rise or stay up late to find out what goes on when you're sleeping.

The important idea is to play in life, giving of yourself. You want to do little things that make you feel good. You put a lot of attention on doing the big things, the profound things, but you want to feel good *all* the moments of life. There are moments everywhere that you could fill up with yourself. When you are watching, ready to make up games, the possibilities are endless.

People notice when you include them in your games of Purpose. Not only will they get a lift when you volunteer to finish a job for them, but *you* will benefit as well. You will be doing it for yourself, to keep you aware of really living the moments of your life. If you are standing in line, make up something to do. Speak to the person next to you. Straighten the candy bars. What else have you got to do? Leave little sparkles of yourself behind everywhere you go, and they will add up. They add up to your awareness of yourself and the difference you make just by being alive in your life—all of your life.

STORY

A man was walking downtown for lunch, feeling great about his life. It was raining hard, but he didn't care because he had a glow inside. He had had a successful meeting with a new client, he was making progress with previous problems, and he had remembered to bring his umbrella.

As he was walking, he noticed a stranger standing under the awning of the bakery, stuck, waiting for the rain to subside. The stranger seemed frantic, as if he was in a hurry to be someplace.

Without thinking, the man hurried over to the stranger and asked him where he was parked. The stranger pointed a half block away, in the opposite direction. He offered the protection of his umbrella. The stranger was startled but smiled, relieved. "You've just saved my day," the stranger told him. They dashed to the car without speaking. The man did not get the stranger's name, but the connection he felt inside complemented his already wonderful day.

COMMENT

Games of Purpose are for you. They lighten the otherwise throw-away moments of life. Games of Purpose remind you of how you want to live. Games of Purpose leave you refreshed and renewed because you got into your life.

THE BIG IDEA

You can create wonderful moments in your life by the games you play.

What opportunities did you have today to make your life brighter?

Make a list of games that you could play tomorrow that would be On Purpose.

What games have you created in the past to lighten up the day?

What are your favorite games of Purpose?

Life Work

Telling Into Being

Intention: To know the power of words

TALKING ABOUT LIFE

Sometimes you forget that words are a medium that create your experience. If you carelessly express yourself, you may not be aware of the energy behind your story. A story is an attempt to share some experience that you have had or are having. Your stories have energy behind them, and this determines the accuracy with which they are recreated.

If you are adept at storytelling, you may notice that you have a difficult time clearing up unwanted experiences. You might be thinking you are complete with a situation, only to find it still disturbing you after you related it. There may be other situations where you need to share a problem, just to get it out. In your efforts to get it finished, you may notice you are telling the same story the same way every time. Talking about it still upsets you, and you are unable to get any movement in the effect it has on you.

All of these examples are various consequences of the stories you tell about your content. You create your experience by what you tell into being. As you live your content, your experience of the issues differs, as does the degree of energy or charge behind the issues. Those issues that

You

are

your

story.

you want to dissipate require you to know what you are recreating. What emotions and thoughts are present as you tell your story? How often do you tell it and what are the results of your telling?

When you examine your life of stories, you will remember ones that are old and boring, even to you. You rarely think of telling them anymore. Remember that these were your favorite stories. There was a charge in the telling of them. Now, however, you have moved on to new content and new stories.

One way to complete your stories is to wait several years until they have been replaced with other stories. Or you can tell them all out now.

STORY

A woman had been divorced for several years and still she was able to tell the latest story of how her ex-husband got her. It seemed to be her entire social life. She called her friends each week with a new horror story.

Sometimes her ex-husband would leave her alone and she would be puzzled. She would talk to her friends and realize she had nothing new to tell them about the saga of her divorce. Without realizing it, she would find some problem to start with him, if he didn't start one himself. She never won the battles but she continued to fight the wars. It never occurred to her that she was creating many of these battles because the stories of warfare are very entertaining.

One day a good friend hinted to her that she was telling great stories. They had a lot of energy and they were always interesting. The friend suggested that the ex-husband may not have such impact if she could give up telling the stories. The woman was amazed. This was her life, filled with experience after experience of her ex-husband getting her.

She made a decision to notice what she was telling into being. The next time a problem arose, she kept it to herself. She didn't tell anyone. It was a longer time before the next problem came up.

COMMENT

In the process of time issues do get solved. You don't want to be a monument to any one piece of content. You want to complete issues and move along. Listen to what you say about your life and its content. How much time and energy do you want to invest in troubles? You are at choice about creating experiences, and the energy behind your words is one method of recognizing what your tomorrows will bring.

THE BIG IDEA

Some experiences you recreate by the energy with which you share them.

If you have a story you want to complete take time to do the following exercise. You need a best friend to participate with you. One who thinks you are wonderful and who doesn't judge you. You need to allot an afternoon or evening of your time. You need to be willing to change your mind. You will be sharing your issue to complete it. You will be telling into being a new experience of an old issue.

Step One

(These are the instructions for your friend.) Your friend is to listen to you—just listen. There is a lot of empowerment in listening. Ask your friend to listen without comments, questions, or interruptions of any nature, without body language of any type. When listeners make comments and give advice, they take the story down paths that may have nothing to do with the storyteller's issue. This is your time, so ask your friend to honor that. Your friend's job is to be with you, to lend you energy that empowers you.

(These are your instructions.)
Tell the story full out. Tell every detail you can think of, how it makes you feel, and what it makes you think. Talk about the history, every event that you remember. Tell it with the idea that you may be telling it for the last time, so you want to tell the whole thing.

Step Two

(These are the instructions for your friend.) Your friend is to listen to you with the intention that you be empowered to complete some part of your story. Ask your friend to make no comments of any nature, to just listen to you as you continue.

(These are your instructions.)
Tell your story again. The same one. This time, however, you are telling it with the intention that you are going to get a shift, a new idea, a new insight. You are going to tell it so that you never experience it the same way again. You may need to tell the secrets, the ones you hoped you would never have to admit. You will need to dig deep for this shift. Do what it takes. Maybe in the final analysis all you need to do is love you. It might even be something that you have thought of before, only this time you are going to tell what it takes to get a change. It doesn't need to be a big difference. Any difference will take you down a different path. Tell it into being so that it will lighten you.

Step Three

The instructions for your friend are the same as above. Ask them to listen to empower you, not to give you good ideas.

Your instructions are to tell your issue into history. Use the past tense, "I used to feel, think, be hurt by." See it as an old issue that no longer has a hold on you. Tell the whole story in past tense; tell how you see it now that it is resolved.

The Big Idea

TALKING ABOUT LIFE

Once in awhile you get an idea that liberates you. It is an idea about a situation that makes all the difference to that situation. Maybe it surprised you because you had had many ideas, implemented them all, but none of them had produced results.

A big idea is an idea that gets results. It doesn't matter what the content of your issue is. If you keep struggling, feel stymied or exhausted with trying, you may need to look for a new idea. But you realize you have tried a million things, thought them through thoroughly, and it still comes down to the same old thing—you don't feel liberated about the situation. Now is the time to rethink your issue, but in a different place and with a new objective. You need a big idea.

You will need to look beyond the restrictions of your mind. Your mind already knows how you should solve your issues, and it continues giving you the same ideas in disguise. Maybe you need an idea that will ease your relationships with your children. You could need a job-related idea or perhaps an idea to renew your relationship. How many rules can you enforce to make your children turn out? No doubt your mind has an endless supply of rules, and you can get more ideas from popular magazines. How many times have you changed job descriptions, hoping that would improve productivity? There are tests to tell you how to improve your relationships, if you have run out of ideas on your own.

The reason your mind restricts your thinking is because it has collected judgments throughout your life. These judgments include everything that you believe is important to you. Getting a transformative idea requires free thinking. The kind of thinking that is not curtailed by self-imposed barriers. It requires expansive thinking; therefore, you need to watch for the thinking boundaries you have set. Maybe to ease your relationships with your children you could look at the rules. You notice that they break just about all of the rules you make. Further, suppose you are tired of microscopically monitoring their movements to make sure they obey your rules. You realize that you have notions about good parenting, but you are willing to set them aside for a few moments. Suddenly, you get a new idea. If they continue to break the same rule time and again, maybe, just maybe, you need to change the rule. Maybe you need to ask them what rules they want, what ones would they obey?

This idea may sound irresponsible at first, until you sit with it awhile. Maybe you try it for one rule's worth. Maybe it works. You will be able to tell by the results. Are you liberated? Is the situation lightened? Does everyone feel better?

If you ask all your friends and neighbors what they think of your idea, they will have their own judgments which are limited by the boundaries of their minds. Do you need it? Isn't it difficult enough to try creative ideas, without the condemnation of those you love and respect? Big ideas work more efficiently if you just do them without seeking approval. It takes courage to get the big ideas in your life. You need to risk implementing them. But, if you are willing to look beyond the limitations of your mind, you will find the big idea that liberates you.

STORY

One day after visiting the school principal for the third time about her teenage son's truancy, a mother felt at her wit's end. She had tried everything to instill within her children a desire for a good education. During their formative years, she had made sure that they had available to them all of the latest gimmicks, guaranteed to stimulate curiosity and interest in learning. She had participated in PTA, scout groups, and was room mother. She had always believed that perfect attendance was one key to a successful education, and she had strict rules about it that promised severe discipline if violated.

The oldest children never gave her any problems, but this youngest son tested her to her limits. He was good about most things, but when he didn't feel like being in school, he was trouble. She had carried out her promises of discipline, grounding him regularly, withholding his allowance, taking away social privileges, restricting his phone calls. The more he was punished, the more rebellious he became. The situation was deteriorating.

She decided to have a talk with him, without putting him on the defensive. She said to him that it was obvious he didn't want a good education, thinking that this would open up communication. The son told her not to assume what he wanted in terms of his education. She was startled by his remark and asked him to explain. After some coaxing, the teenager told her that on some days he just couldn't cope. There was always pressure on him, from his peers, from his parents, teachers, and friends. He admitted that when he was truant, he just went to the park to be by himself and think. She was astounded. She began to wonder how she could help. She couldn't stop thinking about it because they had not come to a resolution.

Finally, she got an idea. She knew that she loved this son and was on his side. He had always seemed a little peculiar to her because he was so sensitive. She wondered if this had anything to do with his problem. She approached him again with her idea. She said that she was willing to let him decide what days off he needed. If he needed time out, she believed it was to rejuvenate himself rather than to be rebellious. The young man was liberated. He assured her that he wouldn't abuse her offer. The rest of the year he asked for five days off. Those days he spent quietly in his room, getting caught up, resting, and doing other things that restored him.

COMMENT

Your mind has a tendency to be repetitive with ideas that should improve situations. That is because it has old judgments. Give yourself the freedom, without judgments, to think up ideas that result in your liberation.

THE BIG IDEA

Big ideas liberate you. You discover them beyond the limited boundaries of your mind.

What situations do you need big ideas about?

What ideas could you have that would liberate you?

What are your limitations?

What big idea did you share with someone that they talked you out of?

To Choose—To Be Chosen

Intention: To claim your Life Work

TALKING ABOUT LIFE

Life Work. To choose it. Historically, only the few saw a glimpse of it. Only a few caught the passion of it. Only a few thought to think about it. Only a few chose it. Chose *to think—to say—to be*—a person with a Life Work—a person with the work of a lifetime.

Life Work. To be chosen. To have the heavens open, to have the universe tap on your shoulder calling you to a Life Work. There are moments when the heavens open and someone is dramatically selected for a Life Work. More often, being chosen is a whisper in the stillness. Being chosen arrives without fanfare.

Life Work. This is where it begins, with the glimmer of knowing that you were born for something. Knowing that you choose it, and it chooses you.

Unlike Life Purpose, Life Work does not naturally and spontaneously appear. It is often not identified as concretely as Life Purpose. For most people, it arrives undramatically. It arrives in quiet whispers. You may realize that you have caught ahold of something. You have a glimpse of an idea, message, image, or the like. You find yourself thinking about it at odd times. Sometimes it is impossible to even say what it is, for although you know you are grasping the tail of something, you don't know what is at the other end.

When you do have a glimpse of it, keep it as fully alive as you can. Talk with others about it. Hang out with it. Think about it. Start doing things about it. Your energy will either sustain itself or it will slowly fizzle out. The important thing is to keep pursuing it, however you can.

Be on guard about your mind at this point, because your mind wants to jump in and squash the entire thing. Your mind might say something like, "Oh, I can't be a wildlife photographer because I live in the middle of Chicago." This is your mind, racing in to stop your pursuit. Charging in to say, "You can't." Be on guard.

Keep it alive in your life. Notice where it has the most energy, and stay with those areas and see where they lead. Stay unattached to any particular outcome. Know that there may be many, many starts. Keep looking for what's next. Do what's up about it. Do what's next about it.

STORY

A man whose Life Purpose was "to provide" was constantly working on ways to start his own business. He was a foreman in a factory and was always looking to see how the business was run. He had a dream that he would create a business that would provide for his family well into the future.

He taught himself what he needed to know and used the skills he already had to begin manufacturing tools. At first he rented the neighbor's garage and worked there in the evenings and on weekends. He was determined to create the highest quality tool available.

After fours years of laboring after hours and after two bankruptcies, he developed the perfect tool and put the manufacturing process in motion. Although he worked enormous numbers of hours each week, he was truly enjoying his life. He could see his dream becoming reality. He knew that this business could be the means to express his Life Purpose of "providing."

COMMENT

If you wait for the heavens to open or the fanfare to begin, you may miss the calling of your Life Work. You can start the work of your life with the smallest hint to build on.

THE BIG IDEA

You are at choice. Choose to follow the idea that "I was born for something."

When have you had ahold of the tail of an idea?

How did you actively pursue it?

How has it grown?

What ideas has your mind said no to?

How are you keeping the idea of Life Work alive in your life now?

What Is Life Work?

Intention: To describe Life Work

TALKING ABOUT LIFE

Life Work has two major ideas. One is that you want and need to spend the majority of your life working. The second is that you want to make a contribution; you want to leave a piece of your life behind. When you consider these ideas you will notice that Life Work is similar to a calling. Not an esoteric calling, but a voice inside that asks you to look deliberately at your life.

Separate, for a moment, your need to have an income and your desire to make a contribution. The market is competitive in the world of work. What you are qualified to do and what you would love to do may be worlds apart. You may feel your capabilities are greater than your present job circumstances, and this is where you will want to begin making choices. You will want to look at your present status and decide which path you are going to follow or if there is some way you can incorporate each path. Can you create a work you feel called to do and receive financial reward for your efforts? Can you maintain your present vocation and still devote yourself to a Life Work?

When you begin to consider a Life Work, you will want to focus on that which will fulfill you.

Life Work has a passion about it. It has a sustaining energy. It seduces you. It won't leave you alone. You think about it wherever you are, whatever you are doing. It will be something that you consider to be meaningful, productive, and exciting work.

Life Work is the expression for your Life Purpose. Your Life Purpose is the driving force that wants to make a contribution. It entices you to keep looking, to keep choosing that which creates your experience of being born for something. Life Work is that voice inside of you that says your life is not over *until* it is over. Do something that makes a statement about your life. Give of yourself fully, all through your life.

Unlike Life Purpose, Life Work is a choice. When you discovered your Life Purpose you realized that you have always had this gift. You do it naturally and spontaneously. Life Work is your choice, to create a great expression for your Life Purpose or not. It will begin to manifest when you choose to do something that is meaningful, productive, and fills you with joy.

There are people like the Queen of England, the Dalai Lama, and others who seem to be born into a Life Work that is recognized and supported from birth. However, most people must search and listen for a calling. You can begin by acknowledging yourself as someone who has a gift of power, and this power lives in your Life Purpose. You can watch for the expression of it that fills you up. You can ask your Purposed Self what it wants to do and honor that. You can start saying yes to those situations that interest you. You can believe that it is never too late to make your entry into life.

The search for your Life Work begins with imagination. Think of yourself with unlimited possibilities. You want a work that will enable you to express your Life Purpose because those are the moments that make you feel so wonderful. So, let your imagination begin to serve you. Think of the ways you now make a difference or would like to make a difference. Imagine yourself doing something right now. Nothing is stopping you. You are the director of your life. Maybe you want to write a book, sail around the world, lead a peace movement, or influence your community. Maybe you want to create a piece of art or be the president of a corporation. Every idea has possibilities. Every creation has an original idea behind it.

STORY

A lawyer found himself in a challenging situation. He had a growing family to support, a legal practice to build, and a fascination and talent for writing. His fascination with writing, however, was in the area of science fiction.

The dilemma was clear—continue to work as a lawyer and retain security or spend more time writing. Any time spent writing would take time away from his legal practice because he did not want to spend any less time with his family.

His value system said that since he had a family, he must do the responsible thing. But, however hard he thought about this issue, he could not get himself to love his legal career. On the other hand, he was also unable to leave it. What about all the education and years of work to get to this point?

If he actually told the truth, he knew that he had lost his interest in the legal field. Without a passion, he was only being a lawyer halfheartedly. He began to notice that from the place of no passion, he was unable to create fulfillment in his life.

COMMENT

Libraries are filled with biographies and autobiographies that document the Life Work of people, famous and not so famous. You yourself probably know people who are involved in a Life Work. Doing your Life Work is different than finding fame and fortune (although some who have fame and fortune are doing Life Work). Life Work means aligning with your life as powerfully and accurately as you are able. It is about creating your life so that all your moments are filled doing the Work of your life.

Life Work is a head space. It is living from the premise that you are about *something* in this lifetime. That *something* is your Life Work.

THE BIG IDEA

Recognize yourself as someone who was born for something, as someone with a Life Work.

As you answer the questions below do not limit yourself with logic. Do not think to the answers. Write down what comes to you. This is not a test—this is a search. You want to find the beginning of a Work that will sustain you throughout your life.

Let yourself relax.

Imagine yourself as someone special.

Enjoy the attention you are giving yourself.

Breathe deeply and relax further.

See your life as a journey manifesting in a Work.

Feel the challenges and the rewards.

What is your Life Purpose?

How are you sharing your Life Purpose right now?

What is important to you about your Life Purpose?

In the world of causes (the peace movement, Save the Whales, political issues, women's issues), where would you love to express your Life Purpose?

How many job descriptions can you think of where you could express your Life Purpose?

If you could do anything to share your Life Purpose, what would you do?

What are your favorite topics, the ones that cause you to notice a charge of excitement and lightness?

What could you begin to create as an expression of your Life Purpose that doesn't exist now?

What ideas do you have that would contribute to or enhance the resolution of world issues?

What does Life Work mean to you?

How would you love to express your Life Purpose?

What job could you have, which would express your Life Purpose, that you could call your Life Work?

What are the details of your Life Work that you already know?

What is your Life Work?

Your Content Is Your Teacher

Intention: To explore your content

TALKING ABOUT LIFE

What you want to do is become fully who you are capable of becoming. Search around for ways to facilitate that growth. There are all kinds of ways. One way to encourage and guide your own growth is through your deliberate attention, such as enrolling in courses that help you sort through your life. Identifying and naming your Life Purpose is one experience that helps people grow. Attending seminars on different aspects of personal growth is another means, if those seminars are directed beyond your personality to your greatest self. Getting together with friends can also be a learning experience, if your friends relate to your highest self, to your Purposed Self.

However, in your day to day living, you are also moving along. You know that you learn much about living just by living. You look back at your life and realize that a particularly difficult time had its value—that you learned. However, waiting for events to happen and for time to process them is a slow way to learn.

There is something to do that is much more active and On Purpose. There is something to learn today, this very moment. If you want to move along in your life, the place to look is here and now. What is here in your life at this very moment? Your teacher doesn't live next door, in someone else's life. It lives in your life, at this very moment. Your content is your teacher. It lives at the same address you do. Look at your own content and see what is there to learn.

STORY

A young woman was discontented with her life. The only responsibility she had was herself, but she believed that she needed someone else to help make decisions.

She struggled in relationships, constantly finding herself on the rebound. Just when she thought she would be happy, some new issue would start brewing and she would find herself alone looking for a new partner.

Her indecision about her life contributed to her unhappiness. A friend, who was rapidly becoming a serious interest, convinced her to move to his hometown. Wanting a new start, she thought a move might help her settle. His influence convinced her it was for her own good. She packed up, leaving her family and job behind.

Once there, she found herself having problem after problem. She couldn't find a job, and she discovered he was not the person for her. After many months of struggle, she returned to her hometown looking for another new start, but once again she found herself on a deadend road. She was bitter in her disappointment that no one wanted to be responsible for her life.

In her misery the man she left behind convinced her that he had changed and wanted another chance. With renewed interest, she made the same move once more. This time it took her a few weeks to admit that he still was not the partner she wanted.

She didn't return home but she is looking to be responsible for herself. Her content became so graphic that she began learning it is not a relationship, a job, or geography that creates a happy life.

COMMENT

The raw material of your growth is the content of your life. Don't look miles and years down the path: it is right here, right now. In the content of your life is your personal teacher.

THE BIG IDEA

Live your own content fully. It has messages from the universe about your personal growth.

What content is presently your teacher?

Have you been able to discern what you could learn from your content?

How will you use this content to further your growth?

What content consistently surfaces for you to look at?

Living On Purpose

Doing The Next Thing

Intention: To do and do and do

TALKING ABOUT LIFE

"How do I get from where I am in this moment of my life to the realization of my goals and expectations? How do I get from now to when I become successful?" If you are daring, the goal is so large that the path to it may not be imaginable.

Have you noticed how you can't think to the achievement of your goals? There must be another way. The other way to reach bold expectations is to do, right now, what needs to be done in your life. For instance, if the clutter on your desk prevents you from sitting down to create, then you must keep the desk clear if you are going to write a book.

When you have done all the obvious things, even the tough things like starting back to school or mending an ailing relationship, then what? Just do the next thing.

How do you know what is the next thing to do? One clue is that it often shows up as a thought that keeps coming up in your mind. It keeps showing up and you can't help noticing it. "I've been thinking that I should move to a more suitable house or apartment." If this thought, or any thought, stays around, it begins to look like the next thing to do. When a book falls off the

Of

course

you can!

bookshelf onto your lap, you'd better notice it.

Have you noticed how you have great ideas, and your friends have great ideas, and few of these actually get created into reality? Why do you think this is? Perhaps it is because the idea comes and goes and is not acted upon. When you are willing to do the next thing, the great ideas get noticed and get brought to life.

Often, in the beginning, you have to remember to remember to do the next thing. And when you do it to completion and it is all done, then the *next* thing will show up.

STORY

Your first child is off to school and shortly thereafter you are attending your first PTA meeting. It is new and exciting and you are meeting interesting people. You dutifully attend and soon become a committee chairperson and eventually you become the president. The first meeting that you face as president is exhilarating and a bit scary. You institute new programs and truly enjoy the work.

Now, your third child is moving on to junior high and going to PTA has lost its pizzazz. It is no longer fun and the energy for it has disappeared. At this point you notice that when the PTA comes up, drudgery comes up with it and you decide that you are done with this group. Now it becomes necessary to look for and do the next thing.

COMMENT

If you want to manifest the fullest expression of your Life Purpose, your Life Work, do what shows up to do. You will notice that things will show up that will stretch your Life Purpose and give direction and energy to your Life Work. Don't worry; the next thing always comes, if you do what is there to do.

THE BIG IDEA

What to do is already in your life. Do it.

What is there to do about your Life Purpose?

What is there to do about your Life Work?

What is there to do about your environment?

What is there to do about your relationships?

What is there to do about your family?

What is there to do about your social life?

What is there to do about your work life?

What is there to do about you?

All Are Called—Few Choose

Intention: To notice that you are called

TALKING ABOUT LIFE

The lives of people who have an obvious calling or mission in life are fascinating. They are read about, talked about, and sometimes used as a model for living a life that matters. Their lives pose the question of why they were chosen and how they recognized their calling?

You may wonder how they lived that they received a calling. Was it as simple as a dedication to service or to a cause? Was it as complex as living their life without making mistakes? Were they tested and tempted, resulting in a passing grade? Or did they ultimately decide that they were called?

Think about yourself and how you live your life. Would you love to have a mission but you are not sure if you deserve one? Maybe you believe that your life is filled with content that prevents you from modeling yourself after someone with a calling. If you take a position that determines you are not worthy of a calling, more than likely you will be unable to recognize a calling.

Consider this for a moment. You know that a mission is not something that you win in a drawing. Mission is not something that arrives with marching bands. Nor is it something that you inherit from a will. And it is not something

Why

not

choose?

you get from passing a test.

Still, everyone is called to a mission in life. You have had many opportunities that would lead you toward a great work in your life. The question you must ask yourself is, "Were *you* there when the opportunity presented itself?" It requires that you be present in your life, making decisions that are fundamentally about you. It requires that you listen to yourself, hearing what you want and need to support your life in a way that inspires you—that you live in a way that empowers you to do those things that create opportunities for you to give of yourself.

When you give of yourself, you have heard your calling. You are on your mission. Your mission is about you, your growth, your willingness to participate with your life. Are you ready to take the next step toward having more influence? Can you recognize that there is a step waiting for you to take? Are you ready to become the model yourself?

It isn't a secret that you want to live life as a wonderful human being. What prevents you from doing so? What are you waiting for? What are you trying to avoid? Sometimes people think that they must sacrifice their calling because they have families, responsibilities, and little ability to contribute anything. It is a fact that a calling will, at times, ask you to stand alone, without perfect agreement from others. It will ask you to search inside and make constant decisions that enhance your experience of yourself. It asks you to answer the questions, "Is this best for me? Will this help me to present the best of myself?" If there is a personal test to indicate a calling, those would be the questions. They would be about you and your readiness to respond to your truth.

If you decide to choose your life and stay centered within yourself, you will discover that your mission never detracts from the quality of your life. It only enhances it by supporting you to be bigger than your ordinary self.

Your mission will, in fact, guide you. There is a never ending source of personal challenges that directs you toward giving the magnificence of yourself. If you choose to confront those challenges you will give your life over to something much greater than an ordinary life. You will have heard your calling and you will have chosen to follow your mission.

STORY

A woman was a devout member of her church. She was on every committee, and she was still not fulfilled. She did her committee work beyond the job itself, and all who knew her respected and loved her. Everyone realized what an asset she was to the church, except the woman herself. She felt she wanted to give more; however, there was no place left at the church for her to give.

One day in the quiet of her thoughts, she suddenly realized she was meant to open a study center. She knew at first she could use the facilities at church, but her vision grew larger. Although she couldn't figure out all the logistics of her vision, she started. Her vision came to life. She felt enthusiastic and determined. She knew she wanted people to know about the message she learned from religion in the way she knew it. No matter how difficult it looked, she chose to do what she could do. She invited people to form a study group. She wanted to be instrumental in the lives of others, and she had chosen to take the first step.

Choose what you can choose. Take the step you can take. A life is lived one choice at a time.

THE BIG IDEA

To choose to give your life to a mission is a major decision that can sustain you all of your life.

What times did someone talk you out of a calling?

Are there moments that you truly want a mission?

Do you believe that you are called to do something?

What do you need to do to realize a calling?

How would your life change if you had a mission?

How would a calling show up in your ordinary life?

What You Say Is What You Get

Intention: To know that saying is creating

TALKING ABOUT LIFE

What do you say in the world about your Life Work? What do you avoid saying that you would like to say? Our words to the world have far greater impact than we give them credit for. We are telling who we are and what we do into being. The world takes our word for it at a level we pay little attention to. Manifesting your Life Work requires your willingness to pay close attention to what you say about it in the world. You want your messages to your world to be exactly what you want to become manifest.

When you communicate what your intention about your life is, others will align with your vision. When you begin to experience yourself as someone choosing a Life Work, your world begins to see your light, and respond accordingly. Let the world know who you are by speaking yourself and your Life Work into being in the precise manner you wish to be thought of. Who will take your life On Purpose if you say something different than that?

You can create opportunity for yourself by speaking about your Life Work as you want it to be. All of your life counts, and you don't know where or when the most important opportunity will show up. You create the significance of your Life Work. Start today telling your Life Work in the largest way you can think of. Let yourself dream about and envision the impact you want your Life Work to make. How can you make a difference in the life of your work? What do you believe needs to happen about it that would give you great joy? If nothing stopped you, what and how would you live your life? Life Work is a big idea. You get fulfillment and passion when you talk into life the big idea of your Life Work.

STORY

A woman knew she made an impact as a healer. Her job was in the medical profession, and her Life Purpose was "to heal." She was satisfied with her job, yet she felt called to a Life Work that she was unable to identify.

Her inability to identify her Life Work resulted in her trashing her profession and her life. She began to complain about working conditions, which made her feel less important on the job. Soon she could hardly find anything good about her work, and she was telling everyone how awful it was. How she spoke about it was how it turned out to be. Her profession was trashed in her own mind as well as others.

She was thinking about changing professions when she realized that she really loved doing her Life Purpose; she loved helping people get well. To get out of medicine was not the answer. But she could speak about her Life Purpose and her Life Work in a way that demanded respect from herself and others.

COMMENT

The creation of a Life Work happens by your telling it. Tell it to yourself and your world over and over. One telling is not enough. Each telling brings it closer to the reality that you count. Each telling takes courage. Live courageously.

THE BIG IDEA

What you speak about your Life Work makes it clear to you and to others that you are up to something when you live On Purpose.

What are the dreams you have for your
Life Work?

Have they changed through the years?

How will your dreams for a Life Work
expand in the future?

What can you do today to begin to make
your dreams a reality?

"I Don't Know"
Is Not The Answer

Intention: To get the answer

TALKING ABOUT LIFE

So many times you hear yourself say, "I don't know." If this is the answer you gave to the question, "How many miles from the sun is Pluto?" then it is probably an appropriate answer. If, however, this is the answer you gave to the question, "What are you going to do with your life?" it is not an appropriate answer. The problem with "I don't know" is that it stops you dead in your tracks. From this answer, there is no forward movement at all.

When you listen to yourself, you may find that you use this expression often, probably to buy time. It is an illusion that buying time is helpful. What "I don't know" brings is a time-share condo in limbo—in nowheresville. That's where "I don't know" lives.

"I don't know" means "Leave me alone, I don't want to answer." It is the ego's way of wiggling out of commitment. Out of focus. Out of movement. It is at its most insidious when you say it to yourself and believe it. Your ego has taken over and is running the show. From your Purposed Self, you either know or you are out looking for the answer.

Who knows

if

you don't?

"I don't know" is a paralyzing habit of evasion. It prevents you from getting direction in your life from your Purposed Self. When you answer from "I don't know," everything stops. And, if someone says it to you when you ask them a question, you leave them alone. Alone to muck about in the limbo of their own drama.

Living On Purpose is the place of knowing what you are up to in your life. The first step is to realize that "I don't know" is a habit that can be changed. Demand an answer from your Purposed Self, and you will be given one.

STORY

A woman constantly deferred decisions to her husband by saying, "I don't know." Should we go here, move there, buy this, sell that? Her answers were always the same, "I don't know." She thought that was the way to keep peace in her home. After some years she began to notice none of her life fit her, but her life did, in fact, fit her husband perfectly. She hated where they lived, their friends, and their relationship. "I don't know" led her down roads she had no desire to travel.

COMMENT

Your mind latches onto "I don't know" and finds it useful to avoid difficult topics in discussion. What is not useful is that your *own* mind is regularly duped by this phrase as well.

THE BIG IDEA

If it's important and you don't know, find out. "I don't know" is not the answer.

What are the important questions about your relationship that you answer with "I don't know"?

How do you answer the question, "What am I going to do with my life"?

What are the important questions about your career that you answer with "I don't know"?

Who do you ask for the answer?

Are you waiting for the right answer?

How do you feel when you ask an important question and you get the answer, "I don't know"?

When's the next time you will search for an answer rather than "I don't know"?

What do you think you might find out if you did know?

Getting Visible

Intention: To show up

TALKING ABOUT LIFE

Shyness is often the problem that prevents you from showing up in the world. Besides shyness, there is self-consciousness (being so conscious of self that you are paralyzed), fear of rejection, low self-esteem, thoughts of unworthiness and a host of other judgments that keep you committed to hiding out.

Sometimes you believe that fixing dozens of inadequacies about yourself would make the difference. Once you get credentials, get money, get beautiful, get smart, get sexy, get good, get enlightened, get better at everything—then you wouldn't mind letting the world know about you. Perhaps you have narrowed it down to only one or two problems that need fixing before you make your debut. You look good and know it, you are smart and know it, you have talent and know it: it's just that you're not X, Y, or Z.

When you identify X, Y, and Z, notice how your mind justifies the excuses. "This is not like everyone else's life," your mind reminds you. "I have A, B, and C at stake." Do you believe you can creep out only now and then, and still be taken seriously?

To make the impact you know you can make, you have to get visible where you are. Even if you

To see

you

is

to know

you.

believe you are visible now, you can stretch yourself more. You need to confront the difficult ones. It's on the other side of the difficult ones that you find the experience of fulfillment. Getting visible may mean adjusting things in your life to make it easier for you to get visible. It could mean having the courage to face your ego and get visible. You know what the process of getting visible really means. Only you know what the secret is—what keeps you from letting the world know you.

Getting visible means having it be OK that you are exactly who you say you are, and letting the world know it. You may be afraid of the challenge. When you communicate that you have a Life Purpose which requires you to create a Life Work—and others really hear you—you create a serious challenge for yourself. There is hardly any way out. You have burned your bridges, and going forward may be the only way to go. The difficulty is only when you stand still. You must take steps that make you visible. Letting the world see you is letting the world know what you truly believe about your life. There is no mix-up; there is no puzzle. You are who you say you are.

STORY

A young woman was shy and inhibited. During her senior year in high school she met a young man and they fell in love. She was very happy because at last she could identify herself with someone.

They married and within a few years they had four children. The woman had little ambition other than raising her children and taking care of their home. She thought she would be content for the rest of her life.

Her entire life revolved around her children. She wanted to solve all of their problems and make all of their decisions. She had few friends and was always hesitant about joining groups where she had to meet new people.

The older her children became, the more they resented her constant attention and interference. She found herself being excluded more often from their lives. She couldn't understand what to do, but her own discontent was growing. She had spent years living her life through her husband and children and now they were resentful.

Circumstances forced her to re-evaluate her life and her priorities. It was becoming evident to her that she had her own life to consider. She began to get out into the world. She joined an organization that had always interested her and she enrolled in a college course. Her family began to notice her changes. She was aware that strangers talked to her and that hadn't happened before. Eventually, she made friends and she became accustomed to being visible in the world, even though it required her to accept the challenge of letting others know about her.

COMMENT

The only way to find out is to check it out in the world. It's only your ego that's so nervous. When your ego gets that you're going to do it anyway, it moves over.

THE BIG IDEA

When you are the same on the inside as what people see on the outside, you are in touch with your own personal power.

What challenge could you accept that would make you more visible?

Where are you hesitant about getting more visible?

How would your life change if you got more visible?

What do you think your family would think if you got more visible?

How much of your life is passing you by because you remain low key?

It Is Never Handled

TALKING ABOUT LIFE

Take a look at your life. How many times have you found it necessary to repeat? Some famous quotations of parents are: "How many times must I tell you," "Time and time again, I've asked you not to do X" or, "This is the third time I've told you to make your bed, come home on time, take out the garbage, stay off the phone," or whatever. At work, you even find yourself needing to remind your employees about the rules a second, third, or many times.

Also, you are aware that the lawn does not stay mowed, the car doesn't stay fixed, the house consistently needs attending, and the very person that assured you that they would never get angry again is now angry. Are they angry because you thought saying "I love you" once was enough?

Your mind is cunning. It has you believe your life will be harmonious, productive, and fun, if only you could get it handled. But almost nothing cooperates with you in your efforts to be done with it. It's bad enough that you can never get on top of your daily responsibilities and interactions; and there is still your personal development to think about.

Wouldn't you love to make one decision and have it settled? And what about choices? You make one choice and that leads to another and another. Problems are never handled. Do you struggle, trying to get to the light at the end of the tunnel, only to find another problem?

Included on your list of things never handled are judgments. The more you give them up, the more judgments you notice that you have. When you give it serious consideration, you realize the truth of it—life is never handled.

Maybe the question is, "Do you really want to get it all handled?" One thing is for sure—your content will never be definitively handled. It's your mind that has you believe that you can get it over or get it settled. This is a subtle phenomenon, one that keeps you hoping your instructions will be followed and your judgments will disappear. Your mind wants you to believe that there is some triumph in it being handled. If your life got handled, then you wouldn't need to pay attention. You could be an automaton.

You have gotten where you are because you had content to handle. You did one thing and another appeared for you to do. You told the kids the same thing a dozen times. When you realized that wasn't working, you were challenged to find a new way, one that stretched you to think or react differently. Each new judgment you give up gives you space to see the hidden ones. The ones that keep you trapped and limited.

Be easy on yourself. You don't want your mind to limit you by getting your life handled. Be gentle with yourself. Let go of your expectations that you will get it handled.

A thirty-year-old man had a successful career. He had finally reached the income bracket
where he thought that he could relax. He had always had financial goals and he had consistently
met them. He felt responsible to provide his
growing family with the finer things in life. And
now he believed that he had arrived.

One evening over a candlelit dinner his wife
announced that she had seen the doctor and that
they would be having a baby in a few months. He
was delighted with the news because they had
wanted three children and this baby would be
their last. He was confident that his life was
right on schedule. He enjoyed his profession, his
family, and all the comforts he provided for
them. They had the perfect house in the right
neighborhood to raise a family. This made him
savor his success. His life finally seemed trouble-
free.

Unfortunately, his wife was having a difficult
time with her pregnancy. She was exhausted
most of the time, and she could hardly eat. The
other two young children became an overwhelming chore for her because she needed so
much rest. On one visit to the doctor, the
decision was made to have an ultrasound. The
doctor's suspicions were confirmed. This couple
was going to have triplets. This explained some
of her difficulties managing the household. She
would need a lot of help.

That week the couple hired a housekeeper
and looked for daycare for the children. They began to talk about the new babies, what they
would need, what bedroom space they could use,
and who would help out. They would need to do
some remodeling of their new house. Three of
everything that a baby needs would cost a small
fortune. Suddenly, some of the best news of a

lifetime was becoming overwhelming. The thirty-year-old man was feeling fifty. He had reached a fifteen-year financial goal only to find it obsolete. This was not in his plan. He forgot anything can and does happen. Life is never handled.

COMMENT

Move the focus away from getting it handled, once and for all. Just do the content that is presently there to do. Do it without resentment. Do it because it is there.

THE BIG IDEA

Life is not finished *until* it is finished.

What situations have you spent years trying to get handled?

What is your progress with these situations?

What comments do you make over and over that fall on deaf ears?

What is a new position you can take?

How much of your life do you spend wishing it were handled?

What situations could you feel relief about if you accepted that they would continue in your life?

What problem did you finally solve, only to have it replaced with a new one?

What judgment did you finally put to rest only to discover another one?

Getting Off It

Intention: To get off it when you are on it

TALKING ABOUT LIFE

One thing about living is this: your personality and all its attendent issues are only an inch away from your Purposed Self at any given moment. When you are living On Purpose, you are living and making decisions about your life, following the call of your largest self. When, however, your personality jumps in, you are living and making decisions from your ego.

No doubt you can remember times when someone said something or did something and they got you. And, when they got you, you may have gotten on it. How the world looks when you are on it is disgusting, revolting, horrible. You are crazed, proportionately many times more crazed than the comment or situation demanded. Even you know it. But you continue to be on it, shrivelling down into your smaller and smallest self.

Being on it is insidious. If you get on it at work, it is very difficult to walk in the front door of your home off it. On it spreads throughout the cells of your body, consuming your life. It infects all the nooks and crannies where you live. Besides that, it can ruin a night at the theater or a dinner out.

Or it glombs onto you, convincing you that

Getting

off it

is

one position

away.

you are right, that they are wrong, that you want to remain as unhappy as you are because you are right. Being on it is also infectious. It spreads from person to person. Just watch how one person can call forth another person's ego to get on it. On it is characterized by alienation, anger, resentment, frustration.

Sometimes you get off it quickly, and sometimes you drag about on it for long periods of time. Sometimes on it becomes a way of life. If you are on it with your living companions or your work companions, it will consume your relationships and your partnerships. It can fill your home with resentments and grudges and can bring your business to a dead stop.

Getting off it is stepping across the line to your Purposed Self: stepping beyond right and winning and self-justified and all the other ploys of your mind. Getting off it is getting free of the tyranny of your ego. It is getting free to live and make decisions from your Purposed Self.

To get off it, mind your mind. Think about what you want to think about. You may decide that winning may be losing, that being right may be the wrong thing to do. Mind your mind— moment by moment. Try taking a five-minute vacation from on it to see how it is. You might be able to get the truth for a few minutes: that on it is not a place you want to live. Getting off it is done moment by moment, until, in fact, you are well past the danger zone. You will begin to feel a little space, a little off it space. That's where you want to live. Guard it by watching carefully the paths that your mind wants to wander. You can easily get hooked again, if you hop on certain trains of thought.

Threaten your mind, if you have to. Say, "If I get on it, it will cost me $2000 a day. If I get on it, my thumb will turn green and fall off, and I will have knots in my shoelaces for fifty-two years."

STORY

One time there were two brothers. One brother got on it about the choice of a gift for their parents. Although he gave tacit agreement to his brother's choice, inside he was seething that his choice had not been selected. At first his brother was unaware of the problem. However, on it spread and soon both brothers were caught up in it. They attended the party for their parents barely speaking to each other. They gave the gift, a gift that was, by then, without meaning to either of them; a gift, by then, without meaning to their parents.

ANOTHER STORY

There was a little girl
Who had a little curl,
Right in the middle of her forehead.
And when she was good
She was very very good.
And when she was bad,
She was On It!

COMMENT

You only get off it inside, because that's where off it lives. When you notice that you are on it again, get off it. The sooner you get off it, the easier it is.

THE BIG IDEA

The name of the game is get on it, get off it, get on it, get off it. It's all in your mind.

To get off it, trick your mind, if you have to.
Here is a recipe for getting off it.

The Rules:

You must be willing to be intentional to start.
You must start to be willing to be intentional.
You must intend to be willing to start.

The Steps:

Close your eyes.
Circle three times to the left.
Get down on the floor.
Get clear.
Say, "I am standing up off it!"
Stand up.
Circle three times to the right, saying:
    "I am off it.
     I am off it.
     I am off it."

Repeat recipe until successful.

Whose Life Is It?

Intention: To know what to do

TALKING ABOUT LIFE

Sometimes a particular issue becomes extremely difficult to live with. It could be a relationship that is at best unsatisfying. Maybe it is an unrewarding career. Various issues make up the content of your life, and your experience of the content determines the quality of your life.

When you learn that you have 100% responsibility for the quality of your life, you may want to reconsider your content. Take a look at your relationships. It is not that relationships should never have trouble, but what is your experience of their quality? Consider the total picture. Who has the final word about how you are and what you do? How many times do you make a decision for reasons other than what the decision would mean to your living fully? Or how many times do you just give up and give in?

Maybe your partner expects you to be a certain way, such as organized, blond, or less interactive. There is nothing wrong with any of these ways unless they are *not* how you are. Maybe you have black hair and you dyed your hair blond for your partner. Do you love it? Does it add quality to your experience of yourself?

Or maybe after working all day, you are expected to come home to a house full of chores. If

Do it

the way

you

want.

you feel wonderful about doing them, fine. There is no problem. However, if you realize you need a long walk and a little private time, how do you feel when someone else determines what you should do when you get home from work?

Living your life the way someone else determines it invites resentment. Of course you want to be a partner. It's appropriate to share details of living. Some details you would do whether you were in relationship or not. But decisions about your personal content sometimes have little to do with your partner. You know what nourishes you, or at least you want to find out.

You can determine what adds quality to your life by being responsible first to yourself. Do you want to pursue an education or career to upset your partner or is it for your own satisfaction? Just what is important to you if you view your life as the most important life you can live?

You may notice that you have sacrificed large portions of your life for someone else and they have forgotten to appreciate you. When it gets critical, they don't even like you and you don't even like them. What have you gained for yourself in terms of the quality of your life? Every time you ask permission, advice, or instruction—be cautious. Are you handing responsibility for your happiness and contentment over to someone else? Who will you blame if it doesn't add quality to your life?

This life is about you and what it takes for you to live On Purpose. It takes courage to be totally responsible for your experiences. It is an illusion that another person can take you on your journey through life. You must decide that you want to do whatever it takes to make your days and nights the best they can be for you. You want to be at peace when day is over. You want to look back on your day and know that anyway you were was about you. You were doing what you needed to do to add quality to your life.

When you are responsible for you first, it is an enormous task. You will become aware of yourself and decide what additions and subtractions are necessary to peacefully love you. It will require you to take time to understand yourself and your motivations. There will be judgments about yourself and others that you will want to be on guard about. You will incorporate into your life those things that nourish you. Your first consideration will be, is this decision about my life, my personal journey? And more than anything else, you will learn that you are about the business of loving you.

If you notice that you personally have done everything to please someone else, check to see if you are turning over responsibility. Did you agree when you didn't? Did you sacrifice and end up angry? Did you keep quiet when you had an opinion? Are there times that you thought you were being the way someone else wanted you to be, only to have it explode in your lap?

After all is said and done, you will change inside to bring you peace. Your life will make a statement that you have love and compassion for yourself. You and how you experience your life will be your responsibility. Then peace will come and you will realize that all there really is to do is live On Purpose.

STORY

A young man wanted to join the Marines. His parents strongly opposed his desire and wouldn't sign the necessary papers. He finished his last year in high school, maintaining his desire and hoping to win their approval.

Every time he brought the subject up, it was met with silence or it started an argument. His parents were determined that he was going to go to college because he was an excellent student. They believed his potential was far beyond what he was choosing to do.

The young man's frustration grew. He took college entrance exams but he couldn't get interested. When his birthday approached, he secretly went to the recruiting station and took the entrance test. When he told his parents what he had done they were angry. They had done everything to discourage this choice and their son was still persisting.

The day came when the young man could sign the contract himself. He went to his parents and gently told them that he had researched his plan; it was still what he chose to do. He explained that he hadn't made this decision to disappoint them. He had realized that it was his life, and he really wanted their good wishes.

COMMENT

Always your decisions are your responsibility. You can get all the opinions and judgments you want and hear all the arguments. But when it's over, you're the only one left who has to live with your decisions. *You* are responsible for your experiences. It is your life.

THE BIG IDEA

This life is your journey, and the only thing for you to do is live On Purpose.

How much of your life is someone else's responsibility?

What things do you do hoping to make someone be a certain way with you?

What things do you do that are about your living On Purpose?

What things do you need to change to facilitate your living On Purpose?

If you change some things, will someone else take it personally?

Will that prevent you from changing them?

If it does, who will be responsible?

The Joy Of Serving

Intention: To realize that giving is receiving

TALKING ABOUT LIFE

Once in awhile, someone does something for you because you are there. They saw your need and wanted to fulfill it. Maybe they felt good about themselves and wanted to share it. Whatever the reason, you received something without the feeling that you now owe them something.

On a larger scale, the world has witnessed people who have performed great services. What moved them to make such a powerful impact? Do you believe they were driven, called, or forced into service? You can begin to understand their motives when you see service as something you do for yourself.

Consider service as an activity of empowerment. It is a kindness or a courtesy or a sharing that originates from your Purposed Self. It does not demand a reward, the reward is in the serving. When you give your greatest self without expectations, you empower others and you are empowered. You are their benefactor and you receive fulfillment. You realize your power and strength. You know your potential.

Do not let your mind be frightened by the word "service." This is not a lesson in servitude that makes you feel trapped. Serving is not simply responding to instructions and demands that have nothing to do with your Purposed Self. You will know the difference by the way you feel. It will be something you want to do for its own reward, not because it is expected. You won't be doing it to please others or to get approval. You will recognize it because it brings you joy.

Great days are created by serving. The fact is, you have the opportunity to serve constantly. It is the place of giving beyond duty or expectation. You are at choice about it. It says something about you. The most fulfilling and satisfying place to serve from is from your Purposed Self, and service expresses your Life Purpose.

When you serve to give the gift of your Life Purpose, you gather an energy about you. This is an energy that supports you to stretch yourself—it wants to connect you with a Life Work.

Think of people who have given great service throughout time. What made them special? Any one of them would probably tell you that they had fulfilling lives. Their concern was not the content of their lives, but what it was they could give to life. It is the consistent issue of wanting life to have some meaning, a manifestation, some great joy. Forget your "Yeah buts." Start today, giving where you can. Do it without charge. Do it because you want to serve, you want to empower. That's all.

STORY

A woman who had been extraordinarily generous with her time and energy became unhappy about her life. Her friend suggested that perhaps she was unhappy because she had become a doormat. The woman decided that she would no longer be used as a doormat.

As time went on, the woman became even more unhappy. She was no longer volunteering. She felt that she had stopped being a doormat but, to her surprise, this did not make her feel better. She would think back on the times when her life was full of generosity and involvement and remember how good it felt to give—to serve. Before she became unhappy and felt herself a doormat, she was actually loving her life. She knew that her energy and presence gave many people the critical boost they needed.

Why had she decided that her service was diminishing the quality of her life? Now that she wasn't doing it anymore, she saw her serving as the very thing that made her feel good. Without it, she had nowhere to give of herself. She realized that it was this giving that called forth the best of her. She began to notice that her presence actually made a difference in people's lives, and this made her feel great about herself. She rediscovered, "To give is to receive."

COMMENT

Nearly everyone's work life as well as personal life has some aspect of service in it. And everyone wants to feel good about themselves and their work. This is the secret to fulfillment—in giving service the goal is empowerment.

THE BIG IDEA

Service is a blessing, not a burden.

How do you serve that gives you great pleasure?

Do you notice anything about your Life Purpose when you serve?

How would you like to serve?

What prevents you from serving?

When did you last serve someone for no reason?

Providence Aligns

Intention: To be open to guidance

TALKING ABOUT LIFE

It is not necessary for you to believe or understand this section. You will recognize the information as fact during the process of living your life.

Living On Purpose means giving up your judgments and doing the things that lighten you up and help you come to choice. Miracles happen when you get to clear choice and make your decisions from there. When you are at choice you are experiencing being On Purpose, and an invisible Source begins to align with you.

First you must get to choice. *Your* choice. You cannot fool yourself about this one. Remember, your personality has a big investment in what decisions you make about your life and how you plan to be. You must always be aware whether you are deciding because you have judgments or if you are coming to choice because you have recognized what is.

When you do recognize what is and come to choice, you make decisions from that space and not from ego or judgment. Everyday you have the opportunity to make decisions about your life living itself. You decide, in any moment, if you want to make a comment that manipulates or controls. You decide if you want to respond in a way that empowers or diminishes. You decide if you want to feel great about yourself and others. You decide if you will continue to be withdrawn or be open and risking.

Providence is waiting for your decision to guide you to a life of Purpose. Providence is an energy that gives you wisdom, power, and strength. Remember times that you tapped into an inner strength that you didn't realize was possible? Maybe you expressed some wisdom that you didn't know you had. Or maybe you recognized that your personal power made a difference that surprised you. Providence is always working to get your attention to support your living a greater life. Miracles happen when you make decisions that are about *you*.

So often you make decisions that support some vague idea of who you"should" be or what would be right. These are the judgments that prevent Providence from aligning with you. Consider those times you were lost and all you could do was plunge through the forest without a map. Something got you through and maybe you thought it was a miracle. It was Providence aligning with you, supporting your own inner strength and personal power.

Providence is a profound energy that is always waiting for *you* to show up to live your life. Expect Providence to guide you to the light when you choose to live On Purpose.

STORY

A woman's husband died. She experienced an overwhelming sense of loneliness. Night after night she thought about her life and what her husband would want her to do. In the deep corners of her mind she kept thinking that she should sell her house and travel. There were places they had always planned to visit and some part of her still wanted to experience those places.

One day she realized her husband was gone, but she still had a life to live. She decided to sell her home, make travel plans, and continue living. She sold her house for more than she had thought possible. She received a job offer that included the travel she wanted to pursue. Her life began to expand because she came to choice and made decisions about living her life. Providence stepped in to align with her.

COMMENT

Providence is a profound energy source that guides you toward the life that you know you were meant to live. Providence supports your wisdom, inner strength, and power.

THE BIG IDEA

When you have the courage to come to choice about your decisions, Providence aligns with you.

What times were you able to accomplish something that surprised you?

What miracles have happened in your life?

What specific times did troubles miraculously fall out of your way?

What choices do you presently recognize?

Noticing

Intention: To stay in touch

TALKING ABOUT LIFE

If you have begun creating the space of living On Purpose, there is something you are becoming aware of. There is a quiet voice that guides you. This voice speaks to you, gently encouraging you to notice how you are experiencing your life. And it will be your best friend, reassuring you that you can live to your advantage.

The motivation of this voice is to help you notice your actions, your content, and your life process. Remember those times that you noticed there was a problem. Maybe someone was angry or frustrated and you didn't acknowledge it. How far did the issue accelerate before you realized there was trouble? If you could look back, would there be subtle evidence that trouble was coming? If you had been noticing, you might have heard your quiet voice guiding you, helping you come to choice. It might have suggested that you solve the issue the moment it began. It might have convinced you that it wasn't your issue at all—that it was really someone else's concern.

Noticing helps you intercept content that doesn't belong to you. How many times have you jumped into some other person's content and lost your intentions for yourself? If you had been noticing, your quiet voice might have advised you to let go without attachment or to look before you jumped.

Another way noticing assists you is by recognizing your experience. You want to follow the path of least resistance, doing that which lightens it for you. If you never notice your experience, you might find yourself struggling and burdened. If you had noticed, you would have recognized that heaviness was looming.

You must be present in the moments of your life to notice. You rivet your attention when you are having interactions, you stay awake when content arrives, you feel the subtle vibrations of the moments. When you recognize a shift is taking place, you are alert and looking for your choices.

It's not difficult if you remember that when you fell in love you noticed everything and more. You noticed how you felt, how they felt, what they were doing, what you were doing, what to anticipate, what was needed, and what was wanted. Many times you knew what they were thinking and how it related to what you were thinking. Your quiet voice was on the job watching out for you and your interest in your new love.

You know you are capable of intense attention. So what you need to do is turn that same attention to your life. Suddenly, you will notice that a voice begins to guide you toward those things that are important to you.

A man was very content living his life. He loved his wife and enjoyed his work. Most Friday nights, he played cards with his friends and on weekends he went to sports events.

He knew he could count on his wife to maintain their comfortable home. She had a career, but he knew she also loved to work around the house, making it just right. She never complained when he wanted to vacation with his friends. He thought it gave her the opportunity to visit her relatives.

One day she came to him and explained that she wasn't happy. She said that when they fell in love, she felt important to him. He would make sure she was included in his life. She told him that recently she had realized everyone and everything was more important to him than her. She asked if he realized how separate their lives had become. In fact, she told him, she wanted a separation.

He was stunned because he had never noticed that anything was wrong.

COMMENT

When you notice your life, you are in charge. A quiet voice points you in the direction that you want to go. If you forget to notice, your life can get out of control. Someday you might awaken to content you don't like, experiences that make you unhappy, and a life that is slipping away.

THE BIG IDEA

You know what you know because you noticed. If you want to know more, notice more.

What problem did you notice before it became overwhelming?

What issues are you working on now that wouldn't be there had you noticed?

What have you noticed about yourself or your content that you would like to do something about?

How will your life change if you notice?

The ending

is

the beginning.

Living On Purpose

The Ending

The end of the journey is really just the beginning. It is the beginning of an idea that you have a great life to live. You have a contribution to make and you have the choice to make it when and where you want. You are the guide and your life is your map. This particular journey is one that only you can make. Sometimes it is a lonely journey and sometimes it is a journey without evidence that you are arriving anywhere. It is also a journey toward discovery about the most important person in your life, you.

When you choose to continue on your journey you will find moments of unmeasurable joy, excitement, and accomplishment. It may not be accomplishment that can be gauged outside, by material accumulation. More likely, only you will know the feeling inside that you are here, in this life to contribute wholly to those ideas that make a difference on this planet, and you are doing it. Only you on your own personal journey can possibly know what that means.

We hope that you can use this book as if it were a friend encouraging you to confront those barriers that keep you smaller than you want to be, to be less afraid of the dark nights of your soul, and to cheer you on to contribute and accomplish all that you were born to do.

INDEX OF INTENTIONS

About Phoenix Rising

Phoenix Rising is an idea, created by intention, to teach people to live their lives On Purpose. The Phoenix, a bird in Egyptian mythology, consumed itself by fire after five hundred years and rose renewed from its ashes. We believe that a new story in human affairs is beginning. We are committed to advancing the cause of human dignity and human growth by addressing old issues in new ways.

Living On Purpose rose naturally from this commitment. It embodies our belief that everyone's life matters.

The Life Work of each author is incorporated in the Purpose of Phoenix Rising, which is Transformation. Pat A. Paulson has Truth Life Energy and her Life Purpose is *Catalyst*. Sharon C. Brown has Workability Life Energy and her Life Purpose is *Source*. Jo Ann Wolf has Aliveness Life Energy and her Life Purpose is *Teacher*.

We address the issues of self-esteem, meaningful work, and profound relationships. We teach people to live their lives deliberately.

> The authors present this material around the country. If you wish further information or to be on their mailing list, please write to Phoenix Rising, Inc., P.O. 3088, Glen Ellyn, IL 60138.